ADVANCE PRAISE

GW00600873

"At last! An author who understands that marketers need to develop themselves as people, as well as practitioners, and a book which provides them the tools, insight and wisdom to do both."

SHERILYN SHACKELL, Founder and Global CEO, The Marketing Academy

"*The Whole Marketer* is a truly holistic, practical guide for all marketers who care to make a difference."

THOMAS BARTA, Founder, The Marketing Leadership Masterclass

"Abigail has created an absolute goldmine of knowledge, insights and advice, all under one cover. *The Whole Marketer* is the whole package, looking at the what, why and how across every aspect of marketing, plus sharing a multitude of valuable thoughts and insights from those in the industry today. Not only does it cover the technical skills marketers need; it also delves into the often overlooked, but critically important, soft skills which are vital for marketers who want to become the leaders of the future. A must-read for marketers and a book you can return to time and time again."

GEMMA BUTLER, Marketing Director, CIM

"You will make fast work of this book. It's an empowering and enjoyable read. Abigail provides an A-Z of what it is to be a great marketer, to be your best self and live your best life. Sharing her passion and expertise, in a practical guide to the key marketing competencies that all marketers will need in their kitbag, and asking thought-provoking questions as to how polished your tools are. The self-discovery finisher is broken down into achievable steps that, once pulled together, join the dots between your soul goals and today. A brilliant formula."

MARY YOUNG, Global Marketing Director, Lil-Lets

"This is a great book packed full of guidance and advice for the modern marketer. From technical skills and tips to know yourself better to the skills you need to lead successful, high performance teams, this book is a vital read. If you want to grow as a marketer and advance your career, then this is the book you need."

PETE MARKEY, CMO, Boots UK

"*The Whole Marketer* is an absolute reflection of its author, Abigail Dixon – a practitioner and coach wrapped up in one – whose style and personality easily brings people along on the journey. It's packed full of useful, no-nonsense theory that is accessible and practical, along with invaluable questions to prompt the reader when working out their own development focus. I love the balanced focus on the 'what' and the 'how,' which recognises that to progress and succeed, you need to excel in both your thought and leadership skills. I know many in my team will find this book invaluable as an aid in their development planning and learning."

KATHERINE WHITTON, Global CMO, Specsavers

HOW TO BECOME A SUCCESSFUL
AND FULFILLED MARKETER

THE
WHOLE
MARKETER

ABIGAIL DIXON

Published by
LID Publishing Limited
The Record Hall, Studio 304,
16-16a Baldwins Gardens,
London EC1N 7RJ, UK

info@lidpublishing.com
www.lidpublishing.com

A member of:

BPR ✿
businesspublishersroundtable.com

© Abigail Dixon, 2021
© LID Publishing Limited, 2021

Printed by Severn, Gloucester
ISBN: 978-1-911671-05-3
ISBN: 978-1-911671-27-5 (ebook)

Cover and page design: Caroline Li

HOW TO BECOME A SUCCESSFUL
AND FULFILLED MARKETER

THE
WHOLE
MARKETER

ABIGAIL DIXON

MADRID | MEXICO CITY | LONDON
NEW YORK | BUENOS AIRES
BOGOTA | SHANGHAI | NEW DELHI

CONTENTS

UNIT 2:
SOFT SKILLS AND LEADERSHIP SKILLS

UNIT 3:
PERSONAL UNDERSTANDING

To my dad, who provided such a great example of the importance of being committed and passionate about your work and, in recent times, demonstrating such resilience in battling his illness. And to my mother, for the commitment she has made and shown in caring for him.

To my boys, thank you for allowing me the time to do this. And also to my party of five at work – Nadine, Vicki, Rach, Natalie and Alice.

A special thank you to Vicki and Nadine, who believed in me and this book from day one, even reading early chapters and providing feedback. I'm forever grateful.

Also, to all my podcast guests from Season One of The Whole Marketer Podcast. Thank you for your time and advice you gave to the next generation of 'whole' marketers. Your tips and advice are included in this book.

If you want to find out more on how to gain the support and empowerment you need to build a successful yet fulfilling career in marketing and life, then please go to:
www.thewholeyoucoach.co.uk.

INTRODUCTION

WHY DID I WRITE THIS BOOK?

I wrote this book because I love what I do – I am passionate about marketing and helping others.

My role as a marketer has always been more than my job – it is my passion. Throughout my career, I have been hungry to grow, develop and constantly learn, to be and do the best I can, but I have often found the information on what I needed to know to be patchy and lacking in clarity. I frequently found it necessary to piece ideas together from multiple sources, such as a course outline, the odd capability framework or the latest approach in a trade magazine. So this book is **the book I wished I'd had earlier on in my career**, with clarity on what I needed to know.

I also found that marketing books weren't always practical – they were often theoretical with the odd case study, and not always written **by practitioners for practitioners**. They were rarely written by those who were on the front line, who had cried in their car on the way home and had to face yet another round of feedback from those not working on their brand. Marketing is a rewarding profession but it can also be challenging. This book aims to give you a toolkit so you feel supported and empowered as an individual and able as a marketer.

Therefore, although I will include some theoretical models that I find helpful and use to train other marketers, this book is a practical book. It is written for marketers by a passionate marketer who has been where you have been. It builds on all my practical experience but also my unique perspective as a marketing trainer and marketing and capability consultant, who consults with and trains thousands of marketers from different backgrounds, organizations and industries. This is coupled with my experience as an accredited coach who understands what we need as humans to feel fulfilled. By putting all of this together, we can start thinking about the marketer as a whole – a whole person – and not just a job title with roles and responsibilities.

Personally, this book plays to my **why** – 'to connect with businesses and people by providing knowledge, perspective and drive, so that they are empowered to make change and grow' – and my **passion**, which is to support the growth of the people and marketers behind brands and businesses.

This perspective was fuelled after many years during which I found that, often, when I had trained or advised someone, they hadn't always undertaken all the actions I had advised or that we had agreed. This was not because they were not technically able but because there was **something in them that was holding them back.** This something varied from a belief that was holding them back to being reluctant to step outside their comfort zone to everything else in between. This realization drove me to train to be a coach so I could help further as a consultant, trainee and mentor.

I have found that marketers' technical skills vary from company to company and from industry to sector.

However, one common theme is that **technical skill is only half** of career development and progression. The rest comes from how you deliver and make it happen and the personal belief and mindset to make it happen.

As marketers' remit continues to expand within many organizations – from a support function (communications) to the one leading the organization (commercial) – now is the time to take stock of the technical skills required, and the latest thinking and approaches. You will need to look at the soft skills, behaviours and leadership capabilities required to be successful marketers, identify gaps for you or your team, and discover how to gain personal fulfilment in today's highly pressured roles.

WHAT IS THIS BOOK ABOUT?

The purpose of this book is to be a practical, reflective and thought-provoking guide for marketers, to provide them with a holistic view of the technical skills, soft skills and personal understanding a marketer needs to have a successful and (more importantly) fulfilled career in today's rewarding yet challenging industry.

In line with this holistic view, from me as a marketer to you as marketers, I make use of some models, but in the main this book contains practical advice on what good marketing looks like and advice and tips on how to implement it. The book also contains thoughts, reflections and advice from other marketers and marketing leaders in the industry.

The goal of this book is to empower and inspire you – the marketer – to feel able and inspired to lead your own career, your team, your business and your brand, and the commercial agenda and growth of your organization.

Units 1 and 2 cover the technical tools and soft skills needed to develop industry-leading, successful marketers who are able to deliver sustainable growth for brands and businesses and lead those in their care to deliver.

More importantly, Unit 3 will help you to achieve personal fulfilment in your marketing career and life as a whole. It will do this by encouraging you to gain a deeper level of personal understanding of who you are and what you need through taking stock of your values, finding clarity on your goals in life as a whole, and identifying any barriers or beliefs that may be stopping you from achieving these. It will also give you tips on the mindset and tools needed to make it all happen.

But the truly unique feature of this book is the opportunity it gives you to develop yourself as a person – by being given the opportunity to explore your own goals, personality, values and vision around your career in marketing. By understanding your 'why,' you can follow a career path that is in line with your personal values and that truly motivates you to love what you do and feel fulfilled as a whole person.

WHAT WILL YOU FIND INSIDE THIS BOOK?

The concept of the 'whole marketer' is broken down into three key elements, which are reflected in the three units within the book.

Unit 1: Technical Skills is about the key competencies required to be at the forefront of today's industry and profession. It reflects the role marketing should be playing as the function or team that is leading and delivering the commercial agenda of the organization. It provides a holistic view of all technical skills and the latest tools and approaches.

Unit 2: Soft Skills and Leadership Skills looks at other skills required by marketers and those who lead organizations and marketing functions. The soft skills covered are marketer focused – those that I witness in marketers who have a deep-rooted understanding of their customers, and those that can help to bring plans to life and to the market. This unit also examines the behaviours and traits desired of marketing leaders. It gives practical advice on how to lead, develop and motivate a team, from providing clarity through vision and setting a capability framework to developing plans and providing support.

Unit 3: Personal Understanding focuses on you as a human, a person and an individual. It encourages you to understand who you are and what you live for, but also what you value and need on a deep-rooted level to feel motivated and fulfilled. It explores how you can gain clarity on what you want and your goals, but also what may be holding you back, any negative beliefs you carry and how to overcome them. We will also look at the mindset required to make these goals a reality and some daily principles you can use.

WHAT WILL YOU FIND IN EACH CHAPTER?

Each chapter includes the following:
- A description or definition of the skill, competency or concept covered in the chapter
- Quotes from industry leaders and marketers
- Examples of good practice (and sometimes bad)
- Top tips on the topics of the chapter
- Questions to ask yourself to reflect on your own understanding or ability

- One or more Capture Time exercises to enable you to capture your learnings and reflect on the actions you will take as a result

You will find the terms 'consumer' and 'customer' used within this book; consumer being the user of the product or service and customer being the purchaser. Although the definitions differ, you may find one or other used to mean both in the book.

WHAT WILL YOU GET OUT OF THIS BOOK?

This book aims to provide you with the following:
- **Practical advice and understanding** by not only defining the various skills, behaviours and competencies but also giving clarity on what good practice looks like, and offering practical advice and tips on how to deliver against each of these skills, behaviours and competencies
- **Learning** in the form of refreshers on tools you know, new learning on those you don't, and information on the latest tools, techniques and thinking
- **Career and personal development plans**, including questions to ask yourself to help you reflect on your own understanding and assess where you are and what you plan to do next to develop – these inputs will feed into your career or personal development plans, or you can use them to help other marketers in your team or care
- **Inspiration** from other marketers and industry leaders, whose thoughts are quoted throughout the book, on our role as marketers and how to practise key skills and competencies well

- **A greater and deeper understanding of yourself** and what you need to feel fulfilled
- **Empowerment** to not only lead the commercial agenda of your organization but also be able to inspire and motivate yourself and your team to gain fulfilment

UNIT 1

Technical Skills

WHAT IS COVERED?

In this unit, you will find an overview of the technical skills I believe marketers need to be successful at the forefront of the industry. We will look at the technical skills – the 'what you do'; the soft and leadership skills – the 'how you do it'; and the personal – understanding 'why you do it.'

In *Chapter 1*, we will look at the role marketers play today, how changes in business orientations have affected our current roles and how competencies today compare with what they were historically. This will allow you time to reflect on your current role and where you are against each of the competencies.

In *Chapter 2*, we will look at the key tasks we undertake as marketers: to lead the commercial and strategic agenda, in particular strategic planning. We will look at the process as a whole and how this fits in with the key tasks we undertake as marketers. The chapter will look at how to start the strategic planning process by understanding your current situation and positioning, and defining where you want to get to (i.e. vision, goals, corporate objectives and objective-setting as a whole).

Each of the remaining chapters (3–7) focuses on one of the key competencies: making strategic choices, bringing strategic plans to life through annual plans and tactics, working with agency partners, commercial acumen and setting and measuring effectiveness, and how to develop and leverage insight to underpin all we do as marketers.

WHY IS THIS IMPORTANT?

The objective of this unit is to give you a practical guide and enable you to reflect on your technical skills as a whole. This should enable you to see areas where you are strong, areas you may need to refresh or improve, and areas you want to start developing. We are all works in progress and marketing is always evolving, so this unit aims to enable you to take stock at this moment in time.

CHAPTER 1

THE ROLE OF MARKETING TODAY AND WITHIN YOUR ORGANIZATION

In this chapter we will look at the changes that have occurred within the marketing profession over the years. We will also look at the new role marketing is increasingly playing in organizations and the changes this is bringing about in marketers' roles and the skill set they need. This chapter will enable you to reflect on the orientation of your current business and therefore the role that marketing plays in your organization and current role.

A marketer's role in business has evolved over time from a function that was there to support the product, service, R&D and/or sales function with marketing materials to one that is leading (or starting to lead) the long-term strategic commercial agenda. Regardless of where your organization is on this journey of transforming its orientation, the role you will play in starting, embedding or continuing this change is vital, as is understanding the impact you can and should be making.

> *Modern chief marketing officers and marketers today need to be part artist (to bring out the creativity), part scientist (because of all the data you need to understand and work with as a marketer now) and part politician or statesman (someone that needs to represent marketing to the business).*
>
> **(Pete Markey, CMO, Boots UK)**[1]

This movement has been driven by the understanding that developing a product or service proposition based on an insight – to meet a customer need or remove a pain point – is a much easier task than trying to create or retrofit a product or service or create a customer benefit after the product or service has been developed.

Those product or service propositions that are based on identified customer needs are easier to sell, achieve a higher price point (as they are based on value in the market) and in turn benefit from a higher commercial return. This approach will also prevent you from having product or service features, specifications or price be the only differentiators in relation to your competition. It may furthermore lengthen your product's life cycle, preventing you from being pushed out of the market when another product with a slightly better specification comes out.

INCREASED SCOPE OF THE ROLE AND COMPETENCIES

The marketing function has moved out of the promotions department and now leads the long-term commercial agenda and defines the long-term strategic direction of the organization. It is the voice of the customer. In the past, marketers were given a product or service that was created outside the marketing function and asked to create a sell-in story or communications plan. However, today, marketing's role is to source and leverage insight to lead the development of the organization's product or service propositions and bring them to market, while being financially accountable for their success. Marketing may also have responsibility for production, the customer service department, and the profit-and-loss accounts.

This has meant – fortunately or unfortunately – that marketers' technical competencies have broadened alongside their job roles. Sometimes, marketers find themselves in a role that they didn't initially set out to do. Perhaps they started a marketing career because they wanted to creatively express themselves or focus on communications – or maybe they started out in product development or engineering and never intended to work in marketing at all. Either way, people can unexpectedly find themselves in a much broader role than they intended, with full commercial accountability. Some people may relish the increased responsibility, but others may feel overwhelmed.

This broadened role can result in our time being stretched, our working hours and workload increasing, and our having to constantly acquire new technical skills. At the same time, we may be missing clarity on what is in our remit and scope – and all of this is in a profession that never stands still.

COMPETENCIES THEN AND NOW

I started my marketing career in 2000 and over the past two decades, initially as a client-side marketer and now as a marketing and capability consultant, I have experienced, trained and observed many changes in marketing competencies. *Table 1.1* lists the key competencies. As you read through the table, score yourself from 1 to 10 in each area (where 1 means you have almost no experience or knowledge of the area and 10 means you are highly proficient and knowledgeable).

The wonderful thing about marketing is it is always evolving, really embraces you, keeping fresh.

(Anthony Fletcher, CEO, Graze.com)[2]

COMPETENCY	THEN	NOW	YOUR SCORE (1–10)
Setting and developing long-term strategy	Minimal (if any) awareness of the organization's long-term strategic agenda; sales/forecast-led approach, with one-year annual plans Awareness of the organization's vision, corporate objectives and mission Delivers the in-year plan, but the majority of what is delivered is determined by another function (sales, R&D, etc.)	Leads the development of the long-term commercial agenda of the organization Aids in the development of the organization's vision, mission and corporate objectives; sets objectives around strategy, marketing and brand, ensuring they are SMART (see *Chapter 3*) and interlinked Sets the annual marketing objectives as part of the long-term commercial plan and translates these objectives into an annual calendar of activities	
Strategic choices	Segmentation based on predefined categories Targeting based on mosaic (consumer segmentation model) (agency n.d.), location and demographics Branding seen as logo identity	Use of personalization and AI to predict individuals' requirements Marketing based on traditional (segmentation, targeting and positioning), with greater emphasis on the emotional needs, shared values and aspirations Also brought to life through tribe targeting Different approaches to targeting; namely Byron Sharp, who outlines how brands grow and the approach to go for a mass audience instead of targeting Brand positioning developed as part of strategic planning to serve market segments' and target audience's needs; reflective of customers' aspirations and the tribes they want to be part of; purpose led	

TABLE 1.1 CHANGES IN MARKETING COMPETENCIES BETWEEN APPROXIMATELY 2000 AND 2020

INTEGRATED MARKETING COMMUNICATIONS	THEN	NOW	YOUR SCORE (1–10)
Promotion	Promotional collateral to support sales: PR, events and traditional advertising (press, TV, radio) To support sales Broadcast of one message across multiple platforms	Use of both traditional and digital means (owned, earned and shared) Use of social media platforms and ecommerce end-to-end platforms Annual business plans are led by customer insight; communications are led by marketing to meet strategic, marketing and campaign objectives Omnichannel approach with tailored messaging across touchpoints online and offline, to move customers through the buying journey	
Product	Development of product specifications and communications led by unique selling points	Insight-led development: long-term innovation pipelines for product and service propositions	
Pricing	Set by product development, sales or finance	Led by marketing using insights on perceived customer/consumer value or exchange Reflective of brand positioning Competitive nature of the market Commercial requirements	
Place	Distribution managed by sales or partners	Marketers define the routes to market to ensure products are available to the target audience (across multiple channels) Rise of direct-to-consumer (D2C) marketing and subscriptions	
People	Transaction-based standardized process	Use of ambassadors and evangelism Staff client-facing roles used as brand ambassadors	
Process	Transactional process	Focus on the customer's journey and continued engagement post-purchase	

INTEGRATED MARKETING COMMUNICATIONS	THEN	NOW	YOUR SCORE (1–10)
Physical evidence	Tangible items (e.g. brochures and other collateral)	Focus on the user experience (both online and offline)	
Agency and creative management	Delivered by a servicer provider	Delivered through a partnership oriented around the commercial goals of the organization and the required brand-related activities	

MEASURING AND MONITORING EFFECTIVENESS	THEN	NOW	YOUR SCORE (1–10)
Key performance indicators (KPIs)	Focused on sales and market share	Set based on strategic, tactical and campaign objectives and used to track the effectiveness of marketing activities and investments	
Return on investment (ROI)	Dictated by marketing budgets and based on a percentage of sales Perceived as spend	Budget set jointly with finance to achieve commercial goals Perceived as investment	
Commercial accountability	Awareness of sales targets and forecasts	Full profit-and-loss management, including responsibility for financial areas influenced by other functions, such as production, procurement, sales agreements, and marketing investment and overheads Management of marketing investment to deliver ROI	
Insight	Research and information Third parties used to gather research	Focus on insight – not *what* happened by *why* – by looking at actual human behaviour Commissioning and collection of data using owned platforms, such as digital, ecommerce, customer relationship management (CRM) systems and social media listening Able to mine owned and commissioned data sources from a variety of sources to create actionable insights (which form the basis of everything marketing does)	

If you look at this table and conclude that your organization is still in the 'then' column, don't panic. Some of these competencies may not yet be relevant to you. Equally, if you think you are already almost exclusively in the 'now' column, you might be thinking "What next?" But there are always new ways to expand your marketing practice. We, as the marketing profession, are on a journey, regardless of our stage of adoption or level of proficiency in these competencies. We are one as a profession together.

QUESTIONS TO ASK YOURSELF:
COMPETENCIES

- Which competencies in *Table 1.1* have you practised during your career?
- Which does your current role require?
- Which have you yet to try?
- Using your scores from above, which competencies do you need to develop?
- Using your scores from above, where are you already strong?

The chapters in *Unit 1* focus on the competencies. The chapters might introduce information that is completely new to you or they might act as refreshers with updates on the latest thinking. Either way, I have aimed to ensure that you will learn something new in each chapter and gain a holistic view of the skills it takes to be a leading marketer. You will need to ensure that either you or your team are consistently delivering against or working toward each of the competencies.

We need strategists, storytellers and scientists.

(Katherine Whitton, Global CMO, Specsavers)[3]

Digital is so prevalent and such an important part of marketing that I think sometimes people forget about broader marketing knowledge. This is sometimes not seen as important, but actually it's the sum of the parts that turn a good marketer into a great marketer.

(Gemma Butler, Marketing Director, CIM)[4]

Each chapter in *Unit 1* looks at a competency, explains the competency and the latest thinking on what good (and bad) practice looks like, and asks questions to support you to reflect on your understanding, identify areas to develop and embed these skills.

TECHNICAL COMPETENCIES

Marketers of today need to be able to:

- Set the long-term commercial strategic direction and define growth aspirations to ensure the organization's wider vision and commercial goals are met
- Make strategic choices about which markets to operate in, which segments to play in, who to target, and how to position the brand and business to leverage market and customer opportunities
- Develop and leverage insight to identify and satisfy customer needs and build insight-based propositions
- Use the full and latest marketing mix to bring plans to life and deliver the required customer experience
- Be accountable for the financial return and performance of marketing's investments
- Be accountable for the financial and commercial performance of the business

Marketers must measure the activity they're doing, particularly in today's environment where they are more accountable for what they do and how they do it, where money is being spent and marketers are responsible for return on investment. But I also think that being the champion of the customer in the organization – and having the ability to better use data to build and deepen customer relationships – is a really important part of the marketer's role.

(Pete Markey, CMO, Boots UK)[5]

HOW YOUR ORGANIZATION'S ORIENTATION AFFECTS YOUR COMPETENCIES

Where you are in terms of each competency will be linked to the orientation of your organization, its industry and its sector within that industry. Most organizations have already moved toward being customer or marketing oriented, some are still on this journey and some are yet to discover the benefits.

So what is the orientation of the organization you work for? Consider how you fit into the orientations listed below, bearing in mind that your organization might be a combination of two of these options:

- **Production oriented**: focused on what the organization manufactures or offers, or what it wants to produce
- **Product oriented**: focused on R&D or innovation
- **Sales oriented:** focused on sales only, usually with a short-term view on selling stock wherever possible and taking any distribution opportunity
- **Marketing oriented**: focused on the customer – products and services are developed to satisfy customers' needs

Stand in your power as a marketer – you are the owner of the customer and if a business doesn't have customers, it isn't a business. And that is a very important role. So, fight and stand up for that and don't let yourself be shoved into the corner as a kind of promotional throughput because that is not what marketing is about.

(Michelle Carvill, Director, Carvill Creative)[6]

Following are a few more questions you can consider to check the orientation of your organization.

WHICH FUNCTION IS SETTING THE LONG-TERM STRATEGY, VISION OR CORPORATE GOALS?

A marketing-led organization will lead the development of strategic plans. These plans will be based on insight, market opportunities, leveraging customer trends, setting strategic tasks based on unmet customer needs, defining market segments, deciding on audiences to target and positioning the brand to grow.

A sales-led organization may have a sales plan or sales-oriented approach to business development instead of a strategy of the type described above. This will have been set by the business development, sales or commercial function. Sales or listing targets will be the focus, based on existing customers and how many new listings or customers the organization is looking to gain. The focus of commercial targets may be turnover or profit margin percentage.

We need to blend and recast the relationships between IT, sales and customer experience. We must reframe the role marketing has within the organization so it works cross-functionally. Marketing needs a rebrand.

(Katherine Whitton, Global CMO, Specsavers)[7]

WHO IS THE CHIEF?

When the organization isn't performing and the shit hits the fan, who calls the meeting and makes the decisions? Who holds approval authority? Is it a sales director, a marketing director, a production director or someone else? This often reveals which function is the orientation of the business. If it's multiple functions, then it's great to see this level of collaboration, but who is left with the most actions?

You could also look to the roles of the board members and the background of the CEO. Usually the CEO's background will indicate the lead orientation of the organization.

WHAT IS THE KEY COMMERCIAL OR PERFORMANCE MEASURE THE ORGANIZATION IS CHASING?

All organizations will have a lead commercial measure that they are chasing. This is the key measure that success is compared against. This can sometimes be an indicator of the lead orientation of a business. Potential measures include:

- **Production oriented**: focused on units sold or run rate
- **Product oriented**: focused on units sold of a new innovation, sales of the products of R&D, or product management of units
- **Sales oriented**: focused on turnover or profit margin by unit or account
- **Marketing oriented**: focused on net profit contribution, market share value or volume, brand health, or product management of units

---

QUESTIONS TO ASK YOURSELF:
YOUR ORGANIZATION'S ORIENTATION

- What is the orientation of the organization you work in?
- How has the orientation of the organization changed since you joined?
- Is it changing?
- Does it want to change?
- Are you working for a marketing-led organization?
- If not, do you want to be?
- Could you be the leader who changes the orientation to be marketing led?
- Or would you prefer to work with a team to do this?
- Do you find the current organization orientation frustrating for you or your team?
- Can and do you want to change it?
- Or at least have equal weighting of importance with other functions?

Use the Capture Time exercise below to define your orientation or thoughts based on the information in this chapter so far. Where are you now? What impact might this be having on you or your organization and your role or development? What do you want to do to improve?

CAPTURE TIME: KEY DISCOVERIES

1.

2.

3.

**WHAT THREE THINGS ARE YOU
GOING TO DO TO IMPROVE?**

1.

2.

3.

Marketing and its remit have just got wider and wider over the years. The pace at which marketing works has got faster and the number of things to think about is just off the scale these days. Marketers have to move so much quicker and be so much more agile. Turnaround times have increased, driven by the environment in which we operate and live.

Technology is getting ever more complex, and keeping up to date with that is a huge ask. We live in an always-on 24/7 environment where people want to order and have access to things whenever they want. The demands of meeting the pace of life in which people operate in society have increased and we have this 'on/off' instant 'want/not want' mentality. Consumers have more information, which means more knowledge so they can make more informed choices. Social platforms have made things more transparent and whether we like it or not, they've given everyone a voice.

(Gemma Butler, Marketing Director, CIM)[8]

SHARE TIME

An inebriated sales director once came up to me at a sales conference and said, "You know, marketing is here to support us and do what we need." At that point I was working out my notice before beginning a new job, and the incident confirmed that I had made the right decision to leave and join an organization that was marketing and customer led. The new organization wasn't dependent on a global R&D function dictating innovation and the marketing calendar, and I wouldn't have to create a customer need and retrofit it to our local market. I wanted to work for an organization that was, at the very least, trying to be market led, with customer insight at the heart of brand strategy and product development.

I love marketing – I think it's where the action is. I think so much of the value in consumer goods businesses is built by the marketing team. They hold most of the big strategic levers which separate success and failure.

(Anthony Fletcher, CEO, Graze.com)[9]

QUESTIONS TO ASK YOURSELF:
ROLE DEVELOPMENT

- Which of the competencies above are most prominent within your organization?
- Which of the competencies are present in your role now?
- Which of the competencies might be present in the future?
- Are you happy with the scope of your current role?
- Could the scope of your role be broadened to allow you to build some of the required skills, leading to career development or growth opportunities?

CAPTURE TIME: KEY DISCOVERIES

1.

2.

3.

WHAT THREE THINGS ARE YOU GOING TO DO TO IMPROVE?

1.

2.

3.

CHAPTER SUMMARY

In this chapter, we looked at the role of marketers today and the effect that your organization's orientation will have on your work. We reviewed the key competencies and how they have changed over time, and you thought about how your own skills might map onto the competencies and what changes you might want to make to your organization's orientation and in your role to allow you to develop. In the next chapter we will look at the role of strategic planning and how to start the process.

CHAPTER 2

DEVELOPING YOUR LONG-TERM STRATEGY: OVERVIEW AND STARTING THE PROCESS

In this chapter we will look at the vital technical skill of setting a long-term vision and goals, examine the keys steps and processes involved in developing a long-term strategy, look at the differences between a strategy and a plan, and consider some top tips and things to watch out for. The chapter also offers some of the latest thinking on developing strategy – specifically, from the viewpoint of agile marketing. We will also look at defining your current and future position, conducting a situation analysis, and defining your vision, mission and corporate objectives.

WHAT IS THE DIFFERENCE BETWEEN A LONG-TERM STRATEGY AND A MARKETING PLAN?

LONG-TERM STRATEGIC PLANS

When you create a long-term strategic plan, you look at the direction your brand or business will take over the next three to five years of its development. You define the desired future position (vision, goals and objectives) and the strategic choices you will make to deliver those goals, and then look to define how you will bring the plan to life across the marketing mix. In doing so, you must ensure you choose appropriate key performance indicators (KPIs) and measures of the return on investment (ROI) for those activities to demonstrate that you are delivering on the organization's or brand's goals.

Your strategy relates to the choices you make about delivering your vision. It usually involves understanding how you will approach your market development or marketing choices, which segment of the market you will target, how you will position yourself and what value proposition you will use to differentiate yourself from the competition.

Creating a long-term strategic plan is important. As a marketer, you are responsible for leading the long-term commercial agenda of your organization. Therefore, it is your role to define where the brand or business is going and what activities will get you there. In my experience, developing a long-term strategic plan also means you will achieve greater market and commercial impact, by having clarity, focus, alignment and motivation on where you are taking your brand and business. It will ensure you are being both proactive and reactive regarding the market and customers' needs; you will be thinking ahead to how you are going to win against your competition by carving out your role within the market and sector.

Developing a long-term strategic plan ensures all resources and energy are focused on the end goal, with the various parts of the organization working in harmony. It also provides clarity to external stakeholders, namely your agency partners. There is more on that topic in *Chapter 5*.

Note that a plan for a specific financial or calendar year is not a strategic plan. It is a shorter-term plan that will hopefully help you to deliver your three- to five-year strategy. We will consider this type of plan next.

MARKETING PLANS

A marketing plan contains a set of actions, usually intended to take place over the course of a year, that are designed to achieve part of a long-term or broader strategic plan. As such, your marketing plans should be closely linked with your long-term strategy.

SHARE TIME

I often get calls from clients saying something like, "We need to write a strategy for the next calendar year." I would argue that this is not strategy – it is a one-year plan. It's great that the client is planning their activities and starting to map out where and how they will invest their marketing spend and when they might launch new products or services. They might even be planning to repeat successful tactics from the previous quarter or year that worked well, especially if they delivered strong ROI or delivered against KPIs. However, this kind of plan is not enough. It won't stretch the business unless it is done as part of a strategic review and unless it forms part of a wider or more long-term goal.

I often say that developing a strategy is a bit like planning to enter or attack a country – or, in marketing terms, to define or combat the competition. Consider the following two options – which do you think would give you greater success?

- Pick up whatever you have around you and just go for it.
- Take the time to look at the country, assess what the current situation is like and review the options available to you. What part of the country would be your best entry point? What will you do differently to win against your competition? What do you need to do this? Plan and obtain the required resources and then plot the best course of action to deploy and then deliver your plans, tracking performance as you go.

This is the difference between thinking tactically and thinking strategically. Of course, simply picking up the tools (tactics) you have around you can lead to success – after all, you may be carrying on with activities that have proven effectiveness. However, we should always be reviewing our activities (i.e. our marketing plans) to ensure they are effective so we can change course (i.e. reconsider our strategy) where required.

HOW TO DEVELOP A LONG-TERM STRATEGY

Organizations and brand teams vary in terms of their processes for developing a long-term strategy, brand plan, business plan and other types of plan. For example:

- You may do this annually with quarterly reviews to track performance, every other year or not at all
- You may have a formal process or you may have your direction provided by another function
- You may be well seasoned in the business and brand planning process, or you may be doing this for the first time and establishing a process as you go

Before we start to consider the key steps in building a long-term strategic plan, I'd like to give a shout-out to Paul Smith, as his SOSTAC® methodology has been one of my favourite marketing models for some time. It consists of the following questions:

- **Situation analysis**: Where are we now?
- **Objectives**: Where do we want to get to?
- **Strategy**: How do we get there?
- **Tactics**: What are the details of the strategy – i.e. the marketing mix?
- **Action**: How do we ensure excellent execution of the tactics?
- **Control**: How do we know we are getting there (what metrics will we measure and how often)?

This model can be considered alongside four key resources:
- People (human resources, skills and capabilities)
- Money (budgets)
- Minutes (time – often the scarcest resource)
- Data (the world's most valuable resource)

Put these together with the SOSTAC® methodology and you've got a solid structure for a great plan.

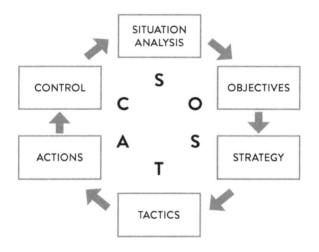

FIGURE 2.1 PAUL SMITH'S SOSTAC® PLANNING METHODOLOGY
(www.SOSTAC.org)

As Smith says:

An in-depth Situation Analysis – covering customers, competition, company's strengths & weaknesses plus trends (uncontrollable external opportunities & threats) is the foundation for a great plan. When you get to setting objectives, developing strategies and eventually choosing appropriate tactics – the answers jump off the page once you have an in-depth Situation Analysis. This in-depth analysis should be half of your plan. You can dump the bulk of it in the appendices if you prefer and summarize it in the front of the plan.

(Paul Smith)[10]

He continues:

When it comes to strategy, the shortest part of any plan, yet the weakest part of most plans, is Strategy. Longer-term plans (5-year plans) tend to have more product portfolio matrices (Ansoff, GE, Boston Consulting, Nagji & Tuff's Innovation Ambition Matrix) to help determine which products for which markets plus matching the company's risk appetite with ambition.

(Paul Smith)[11]

TOP TIPS FOR DEVELOPING
A LONG-TERM STRATEGIC PLAN

Be clear up front on where you want to get to and what you want to achieve

- Spend the time up front to understand where you want to get to and in what time frame in terms of each key measure - both internal (i.e sales out) and external measures (i.e. market share). Later in the chapter you will find an exercise based around 'from and to' statements, which you can use to help you clarify your thinking at the start of the process.

Use creativity

- Embrace creative or design thinking throughout the process
- Inspire creative team behaviour to stretch thinking throughout, not just at the end when it comes to communications, and use techniques that stretch your thinking

Recruit a cross-functional team

- Build a cross-functional team with people from functions outside your category and from outside the marketing department, to give you insight and broad organization thinking and alignment
- Bring in external consultants or agency partners to keep you on course and challenge and stretch your thinking
- Make these external people part of the journey; because they are already bought in to the plan, they will be your advocates as you gain buy-in and roll out your plans
- People who are external to your team or business will challenge your thinking – overcome mindsets oriented around the idea that something that didn't work before can never work again, to stop you narrowing your thinking

Think broad

- Consider macro trends: not just those affecting your category but the customer as a whole (many opportunities lie here, I promise you)
- Also consider micro trends: too many plans outline only the one or two other key players in the organization's category – is that how your customers see the competition, same need but with a different product?
- Consider direct and indirect competition, both inside and outside your category
- Don't overlook challenger brands: if you are one, then keep being agile to respond to unmet customer needs quickly; if you are a larger player, take what learnings you can from challenger brands to become more responsive

- Consider substitutes from inside or outside your category – which brands could steal your customers or consumers with an alternative product or service?

Stay strategic

- Before jumping into the mix of specific activities, gain clarity on the strategic choices you are making – for example:
  › Define which markets you will play in (e.g. geographically, by industry, new or existing, with the same offering or different)
  › Define which segments of the market you will go after (e.g. existing or new)
  › Define which target audience you will go after, or will you target a mass audience (see more on Byron Sharp's thinking on this topic in *Chapter 3*) or even target tribes?
  › Define how you will position yourself and what your proposition will be to satisfy the above

Set and talk the board language

- Use the same lead measure that the business is chasing (e.g. net sales, trading contribution, units or volume) to show how your long-term strategy will deliver against the commercial agenda
- Market share, penetration, frequency, Average Weight of Purchase (AWP) and so on are still important measures, but these are marketing measures and will not serve to show how you are delivering against your wider strategy

Ladder up with finance until you find some common ground. So both marketers and commercial people ultimately have the same role and goal.

(Emma Heal, Managing Director and Partner, Lucky Saint)[12]

Use the whole marketing mix

- When defining how you are going to bring your plans to life, use all of the 7 Ps or all of the 4 Es (covered in *Chapter 4*) – whichever you prefer
- Avoid identifying a category opportunity but then making no strategic choices and orienting your calendar mainly around promotion or supporting product launches – you have control of the whole mix, so own it

Key issues and opportunities

- Yes, it's important to use this process to identify new customer needs or market opportunities that will allow you to grow, but it's also important to have a realistic view of threats and issues you need to address
- I always worry when I see a list only of opportunities – we need to protect, maintain and defend to avoid a leaky bucket (i.e. losing sales while gaining sales, with the result being that we stay in the same position)

Stay true and realistic

- The longer you work for an organization, the harder it is to be objective and realistic about your strengths and weaknesses; think from your competitors' perspective – would they agree with your lists of your strengths and weaknesses?

SITUATION ANALYSIS

The first step of any strategic planning process is to define the current position of your organization and your market as a whole. You need to look at not only what is currently happening but also what is going to happen or could possibly happen in your market as a whole over the next three to five years or for the duration of the plan you are writing.

Start by conducting an **audit of the macro environment**. Macro factors are outside your control but may affect you or provide growth opportunities. You can use the PESTLE acronym (Pestle Analysis n.d.) to outline the external macro factors that we need to look to review during this stage; namely political, economic, social, technological, legal and environmental. Particularly focus on social and economic trends if you operate in a customer market, as these reflect customer buying power and behaviour changes. Also, don't just consider your category but also your customer – what is affecting them and you as an organization?

Now conduct an **audit of the micro environment** (e.g. stakeholders, suppliers, customers, employees and competitors – micro factors are outside your control but inside your influence). Focus on your competition and run scenario plans, looking at not only what your competitors are doing now but also what they are likely to do next, what you would do as a result and what your customers may then do in response.

You should also conduct an **internal audit**, looking at your strengths and weaknesses as an organization or brand in order to capitalize on growth opportunities and prevent adverse events. I often use the McKinsey 7S Framework. The seven elements of this framework – systems, style, staff, structure, strategy, skills and shared values – comprise hard and soft measures. This should help you to understand how well placed you are as a brand or business to meet existing and future market and customer needs.

Once you have completed all three audits, you can pull your findings together in a SWOT (strengths, weaknesses, opportunities and threats) grid, as shown in *Table 2.1*.

Strengths	Weaknesses
Opportunities	Threats

TABLE 2.1 SWOT ANALYSIS

Rate the likely impact of each item (e.g. high, medium or low) – I often do this through a commercial lens so the financial implications are clear. Next you can look for key threats and opportunities. Look to cluster your themes together and prioritize – for example, five in each group.

SETTING YOUR GOALS
AND VISION – 'TO'

'FROM AND TO' STATEMENTS

Having conducted your situational analysis ('from') we can now look at your 'to.' 'From and to' statements allow you to define where you are now ('from') and where you want to get to in a specific time period ('to') – perhaps three or five years. Using your findings from the audits and thinking outlined above, fill in the 'from' column in *Table 2.2* (I have included some examples for you, and you can add your own at the bottom). Then define your vision, aspirations and commercial goals in the 'to' column (there is more on this in the next section). You can check how realistic these are later.

MEASURE	'FROM'	'TO'
Market share	18% value	20% value
Turnover	£1.2 billion	£1.8 billion
Profit margin	30%	30%
Customer perception		
Brand awareness		
Customer penetration		
Retailers' weighted distribution		
Compound annual growth rate (CAGR)		

TABLE 2.2 'FROM AND TO' STATEMENTS

TOP TIPS FOR STRATEGIC PLANNING

One of the first exercises I do when I'm asked to help a client lead the strategic planning process within their organization is to work out what the required brand movement is. This starts with defining where you are now and where you want to get to – and by when.

VISION, MISSION AND CORPORATE GOALS

Having defined your 'from and to' statements, you need to consolidate this thinking to provide clarity on your vision, mission and corporate goals.

WHAT IS A VISION?

A vision is about dreams, goals and aspirations. It is an aspirational statement about what your organization wants to achieve in the medium and long term. Where do you want to get to? Its role is pivotal in providing clarity and motivation for the organization as a whole.

> *When you don't have a vision, decisions that you make on a day-to-day basis become tactical and so you don't see the prize – what you see is the obstacle.*
>
> **(Ronnie Clifford, Owner and Founder,**
> **Real Coaching 4U and Leadership trainer)[13]**

WHAT IS A CORPORATE MISSION STATEMENT?

A corporate mission statement has three main components:
1. The goal of the organization
2. The organization's 'how' – perhaps its core values, and how it plans to behave as a business in order to achieve its goal

3. Why the organization aims to achieve its goals and objectives

The mission must be feasible and attainable.

WHAT ARE CORPORATE GOALS?

Corporate goals are at the heart of the planning process and describe the direction, priorities and relative position of the organization and its markets. They help an organization to determine how it will deliver its vision and specify the key building blocks.

Usually, the 'commercial number' will be found here. This is a term I use for a commercial aspiration, target or lead measure that is reflective of what the organization is looking to achieve, whether that is a profit figure, turnover, a unit number or something else. It is a commercial aspiration that is closely linked to the three traditional components above (vision, mission and goals).

A quantitative number is useful because it provides clarity on what needs to be achieved. It allows success to be objectively defined and reviewed. It also makes it a lot easier to translate an aspiration into annual targets and to ensure each aspect of the business (whether a division, unit or brand) is clear on its accountability in terms of delivering on the vision. You can divide up a number, but it is a lot harder to divide up a general aspiration and specify what it means for each area of the business. For example, the commercial number '£100 million of growth over the next five years' can easily be divided across any number of business units, as appropriate. However, this is less the case for aspirations such as 'double the size of our social media following' – although this is a measurable goal, it is harder to provide clarity across multiple business units as to who has accountability for what.

In an ideal world, your marketing strategy should flow from your corporate goals. Your marketing strategy should allow you to actualize your corporate objectives in terms of which markets to target, which segments of those markets to target, who to target, and how to position your organization over a defined time period to achieve your goal.

FIGURE 2.2 HOW VISION TRANSLATES INTO THE MARKETING STRATEGY AND ACTIVITIES

SHARE TIME

I once saw a vision for an organization that said it wanted to be the most recommended brand. For me what was missing here was clarity on how this vision would be translated into an objective or goal for each of the organization's brands. It would of course be possible for the organization to measure whether it was the most recommended brand by setting up brand-tracking measures. However, the commercial role of each brand or team in delivering the vision was unclear.

Confusion can arise when there is an attempt to add a commercial target into an organization's vision, mission or corporate goals, and it can often cause much debate. Marketers tend to be trained to believe that a vision should never incorporate a commercial objective and that the role of a vision or mission is solely to inspire and motivate employees.

I believe that it needs to do both. An organization's objectives do need to be inspirational and motivational – they need to let employees know why they are being asked to do what they do. However, the objectives also need to give clarity on what the end goal and annual goal look like. Commercial targets have their place in providing that clarity.

Simon Sinek's ideas are useful in understanding the inspirational part of this balancing act.

SIMON SINEK AND LEGACY OF PURPOSE

Sinek is an author and motivational speaker whose work has started to change the way we think about how we communicate about our business and their propositions and set their visions. Most of Sinek's work focuses on

why organizations and individuals do things as opposed to what they do or how they offer a product or service. This is based on the idea that customers are more likely to buy based on why you do something rather than what you do.

Sinek believes that people buy an emotional connection or story – the **why** of an organization – over what it functionally provides. He has written an array of books that focus on this idea of why. His first book, *Start with Why*, outlines how to build brand propositions with his Golden Circle brand proposition tool.[14] *Find Your Why* supports individuals to find their own reasons and motivations behind why they get up every day,[15] and *Leaders Eat Last* outlines how great leaders sacrifice their own comforts for the good of those in their care.[16]

The Infinite Game, Sinek's latest book at the time of writing, encourages individuals and their organizations to think less about the commercial number that needs to be delivered in a specific time period (the 'finite game,' with defined players and fixed rules).[17]

Instead, Sinek encourages leaders to think more about the infinite game – about the legacy they want to leave behind. In the infinite game, the way you deliver your legacy may change and can constantly keep evolving. The idea is that a vision with longevity will lead to an organization constantly evolving and employees who are more emotionally bought into the vision.

QUESTIONS TO ASK YOURSELF:
LEGACY

- What legacy do you want to leave behind?
- What legacy does the organization you work for want to leave behind?
- What vision can you set to ensure that everyone is clear, aligned and motivated to deliver?

AGILE MARKETING

Agile marketing is a process in which marketing teams (or the organization as a whole) strive to get work done and activated in the market. It can be a strategic or tactical approach, but it still requires an organization to have clarity on its vision and on where it wants to get to in the long or medium term. Instead of translating the strategy into an annual plan with a defined key burst of activities (e.g. communication campaigns or product launches), it looks ahead quarter by quarter and breaks tasks or activities down in two- to four-week cycles.

Originating in IT software development, the purpose of agile marketing is to expedite the launch of products, services, communications and so on into the market. This allows for swift customer feedback and insight to inform suggested improvements or iterative changes, as opposed to following a classic customer-testing or 'gate' process, which although robust elongates the time taken to launch a product into the market. It involves using data, analytics and insight to identify market opportunities, and testing and evaluating initiatives in real time.

Agile marketing is about customer-focused collaborative teams who have clear, measurable goals coming together to deliver many rapid iterations and small experiments using testing and data to make decisions.

(Rachel Chapman, Co-founder, Agile Marketing Community)[18]

WHAT DO YOU NEED TO FOLLOW AN AGILE MARKETING APPROACH?

In order to adopt an agile marketing approach in your marketing function and processes, there are six key disciplines or principles you need to follow.

1. Quick response

Respond to the changes you identify on a quarterly or fortnightly basis, rather than blindly following an annual plan. Get into a cycle of putting defined actions in place to respond to changes in the market, with speed.

2. Rapid iterations

These are little iterations (or changes) that are quickly made and launched into the market as opposed to larger-scale, coordinated marketing activities (e.g. a marketing campaign or product launch where a key burst of activities is the focus).

3. Testing and data over opinions and conventions

In agile marketing, all activities are tested, results are measured, and findings are shared so that learnings and ideas about what to do next are captured as actions. Decisions are made based on facts and testing, not on gut instinct and internal hearsay. This takes a cultural shift as decisions are made autonomously by the team (the 'scrum' in agile's terminology) and not by the leadership or according to the HIPPO (highest paid person's opinion).

4. Many small experiments over a few large bets
Agile marketing often uses the following splits to determine budget allocation and to focus on experimentation:

- 70% of the budget and 50% of the time are spent on what we know works
- 20% of the budget and 25% of the time are spent on modifying what we know is working but with a focus on improving
- 10% of the budget and 25% of the time are spent on testing and learning so as to generate new ideas

5. Collaboration over silos and hierarchy
All functions need to work collaboratively with one another. The process needs to span more than just marketing and be adopted across all key functions. Everyone needs to work collaboratively to make the necessary fortnightly changes and to introduce the rapid iterations on which agile marketing is based. The organization needs to create processes to enable people to work in this way.

6. Continuous improvement
The organization needs to adopt a continuous improvement process in which employees are empowered to suggest changes, make changes, capture and use any successes to move forward, and capture any failures as learning – all with the goal to improve the effectiveness of the product offering, communication, service and so on.

WHAT ARE THE BENEFITS OF AGILE MARKETING?
It is **competitive**, due to the speed with which products are launched into the market. Product and service propositions, or tactical activities, can be brought to the market quickly, potentially allowing you to expedite your entrance into the marketplace. This is especially useful in highly competitive

markets where existing players, new entrants (challenger brands) and substitutes may all be present.

There is a focus on **outputs** and clarity on what is being worked on in the here and now. The fortnightly cycle means that less time is spent reviewing and more time is spent on the key output required in the short time frame.

Fact-based decision-making is the ruling principle. Data is collected and learnings are documented to keep the focus on fact-based learning, and there is less room for human subjectivity and emotional attachment to projects and their success.

There is a positive team culture, which should hopefully increase motivation and therefore productivity, as long as senior management is supportive and allows teams to have the necessary autonomy to make decisions based on data. This is based on three principles. Firstly, there is no such thing as failure – agile marketing is all about capturing learning so as to move forward. Secondly, there is internal clarity about what the organization is doing over any given two-week period (organizations commonly use a one-page task sheet to set tasks and priorities for each function). Finally, there is no hierarchy in decision-making – teams have the autonomy to use data to support their decisions.

WHAT ARE THE DOWNSIDES OF AGILE MARKETING?

Changes are made at a low level, which can result in less impactful bursts in the marketplace that may not outweigh competitive noise or gain customer awareness. Also, due to the **shorter time period** for measuring success, nuances may not be considered, such as competitors' activity or the impact of weather. There is a risk of constantly being tactical and not being strategic or building the brand.

There may be **reduced distribution** without the clarity that retailers need in order to list a product in their designated range windows.

People can burn out and progression can stall when people work in intense bursts without a break. There is also a risk of lack of clarity around reporting lines and career progression opportunities.

An initial investment is required in production, technology, data collection, the skill sets needed to interpret data and action it quickly, and bringing in agile marketing experts to train, facilitate, mentor and coach.

Customers may be dissatisfied. Although agile marketing aims to enhance the customer experience, customers will also potentially retain frustrations from a previous experience of a product if, for example, it wasn't robustly tested before launch, causing negative brand perception or negative word-of-mouth and a reluctance to make repeat purchases of the brand's products.

WHO IS DOING AGILE MARKETING WELL?

Case studies of successful implementations of agile marketing often come from tech companies or martech (marketing technology) publications. This is not at all surprising, given (as mentioned above) that the concept originates in the IT world.[19]

The meal kit company Gousto has adopted agile marketing as a strategic approach, part of its blueprint. Santander uses it tactically to meet its objectives and key results (OKRs.)

At Santander it could take literally six weeks to get something signed off because you'd send something out and compliance would have one view, product would have another and then they would come back with different views. So you'd mark it up and send it out again. Now everyone gets in a room together and sign-off can be done in an hour.

(Rachel Chapman, Co-founder, Agile Marketing Community)[20]

GETTING STARTED WITH AGILE MARKETING

Rachel Chapman, co-founder of the Agile Marketing Community, offers the following progression for getting started with agile marketing:[21]

1. Pick a customer issue (something small with a clear objective) that needs to be solved and that you believe you can do something about.

2. Pick a group of people (no more than ten) who can solve that issue and who between them have the right agile mindset (collaborative, focused on delivering value, able to adapt to change and great at putting themselves in the customer's shoes; additionally, at least one team member should have experience with agile).

3. Set clear and measurable goals, and ensure that all team members understand what they are trying to achieve.

4. Let them go for it – encourage them to put together a list of all their ideas about what might help them to deliver the goal and then get started using testing and learning (or A/B testing, where two versions of an approach are trialled to test which is the best) with small iterations.

WHAT GOOD LOOKS LIKE

- There is a clear vision that is not only motivational but also provides clarity about what success looks like and about the commercial number (e.g. turnover or profit) that everyone is striving to achieve
- A strategy has been built with a cross-functional team and has cross-functional buy-in from the start
- Commercial targets have been stated and there are clear, interlinked KPIs in place to measure delivery

---

WHAT BAD LOOKS LIKE

- No commercial clarity or target has been set
- A strategy has been written by the marketing team but then not shared with wider teams, and buy-in has not been sought
- Only opportunities have been identified – not key threats (this is likely to lead to the leaky bucket scenario explained previously)
- The strategy is only used while sales are on target
- No strategic choices have been made – the organization has jumped straight into using tactics (e.g. looking at which segments to target or which promotions to use)
- The strategy contains internal biases (e.g. 'we are great at such-and-such')
- No measures of effectiveness or KPIs have been set

QUESTIONS TO ASK YOURSELF:
ASSESS YOUR OWN COMPETENCY

- Are you able to think long term about where you want to take your business or brand? Are you clear on what this new position will look like?
- Can you clarify this thinking into a vision, mission, corporate goal and commercial numbers so as to provide clarity and motivation for your team or brand?
- Are you familiar with the process of developing a long-term strategic plan (either using existing models or defining your own process)? Are you able to lead others through this process?
- Are you able to apply insight throughout the whole process?
- Are you able to develop a vision that provides an aspirational stretch but that can also realistically be delivered?

CAPTURE TIME: KEY DISCOVERIES

1.

2.

3.

WHAT THREE THINGS ARE YOU GOING TO DO TO IMPROVE?

1.

2.

3.

CHAPTER SUMMARY

In this chapter, we looked at the strategic process as a whole and defined the latest thinking on marketing strategy and tactics, including how to start the process with a situation analysis, how to define 'from and to' statements and how to get started with agile marketing. The next chapter focuses on strategic choices. This is about focusing the organization's energies and investments to actualize the desired vision and commercial goal, and to leverage the market opportunities and defend and maintain your existing position.

CHAPTER 3

MAKING STRATEGIC CHOICES

In this chapter we will look at what strategic choices are and why they are important. We will consider how to set SMART (specific, measurable, action-oriented, realistic/relevant and timed) objectives to provide clarity on success and goal setting. We will then examine the various strategic choices you can make around targeting and positioning.

In my experience, this stage of brand planning is generally characterized by one of the following issues:

- Aspirational targets and segments have been written but are not commercially sized or validated, and are often unrealistic
- There is a lack of understanding among those in the wider organization about what the organization's overall vision, mission and goals are, so specific functions' strategies are not geared toward delivering on the vision, mission or goals

Clarity on strategic choices can help to avoid these situations arising.

WHAT ARE STRATEGIC CHOICES?

Strategic choices are, in a nutshell, choices organizations make about what they are going to focus on. They concern where the organization chooses to invest its financial and emotional energy, and they involve determining where the organization is likely to have the greatest success and commercial gain versus its competition. Where the organization is *not* going to operate is just as important as where it decides to operate. *Table 3.1* provides some examples.

AREA OF CHOICE	QUESTION TO ASK	EXAMPLE
Markets	Which markets are we going to go after (e.g. geographically, by industry, by category)?	French car market
Segments	Where are we going to operate in that market?	Family cars/people carriers
Targeting	Which customers are we going to go after within that segment?	Demographics - BC1 2+, children, families with primary-school-aged children based in suburban locations and who have busy lifestyles. Both parents work and the children have many hobbies and interests. The parents feel overwhelmed with constant juggling of work and family commitments and are reluctant to switch from an executive car to a people carrier. The family values experiences and connection. The parents feel guilty because they don't spend enough time with their children and they feel life is all about compromise
Proposition and positioning	How will we win against our competition?	We will be the perfect solution for modern, busy families who wish to experience life to the fullest in such a way that no compromise is needed

TABLE 3.1 STRATEGIC CHOICES

Strategy is an integrated set of choices that uniquely positions the firm in its industry so as to create sustainable advantage and superior value relative to the competition.

(Alan Lafley and Roger Martin)[22]

WHY ARE STRATEGIC CHOICES IMPORTANT?

Strategic choices are important for several reasons:

- They ensure that your investment of time and money is focused to have the greatest impact and provide the greatest commercial return
- They provide clarity internally on the direction you are taking and ensure anything you bring to market reflects this
- They provide clarity externally with your customer regarding what you offer, where you offer it and what you stand for

Making strategic choices means evaluating the options available and deciding where to focus your resources by reviewing the following and how to deliver against them:

1. The goals and aspirations your wider organization wants to achieve, and its vision, mission, desired legacy and objectives (see *Chapter 2*)
2. Which opportunities are commercially robust and sizeable, and will allow you to meet your commercial aspirations and goals
3. Where you will be able to leverage your organization's strength to succeed versus existing and future competition

SETTING OBJECTIVES

Before you can make strategic choices, you need to set objectives. Once you have determined your desired goal or direction, you can capture it as an objective. An objective is a clear, defined picture of the goal or win you are looking to make. In your strategy, all objectives should be interlinked, each one helping to deliver the others. *Figure 3.1* represents how your organization's vision feeds down to various types of objective.

FIGURE 3.1 THE HIERARCHY OF OBJECTIVES

Additionally, all of your objectives should be SMART (specific, measurable, action-oriented, realistic/relevant and timed). *Table 3.2* explains this further and gives some examples.

	WHAT THIS SHOWS	EXAMPLE
SPECIFIC	Which, what, who, where and why?	Grow the value of the brand's market share
MEASURABLE	How much do you need to deliver?	By 3 percentage points
ACTION-ORIENTED	How will you deliver it?	By stealing from x, y and z competitors
REALISTIC/ RELEVANT	Can it realistically be achieved?	Check that a 3-percentage-point increase will be realistic based on the time period, investment, market, etc.
TIMED	By when will it be achieved?	By the end of May 2022

TABLE 3.2 SMART OBJECTIVES: EXAMPLES

With this level of clarity established, you can further assess your objectives by considering the following:

- **Are they commercially viable?** Are the objectives proportionate and accessible, and is there space in the market (i.e. is it not overly saturated with other competitive players)?
- **Will you be able to win?** Where are you most likely to succeed given your strengths and capabilities as an organization and brand, and where can you leverage existing and future strengths to win against your competition?
- **Do you have the necessary resources and enablers** to go after this space and do you have the investment and resources to operate there?

A great model to use as a strategic starting point is OGSM (objectives, goals, strategies and measures). The model has its origins in the 1950s but one great explanation of it can be found in Alan Lafley and Roger Martin's *Playing to Win*.[23]

BEFORE YOU START TO MAKE YOUR STRATEGIC CHOICES…

I feel like I need to acknowledge that being strategic is easier said than done. I often find organizations are claiming to be strategic but are only looking to the next year's annual plan or using communications to set themselves apart from their competition. We need to have both clarity on strategy and tactical success to outwit the competition. You will find more on this later in the chapter in the section 'The long and the short of it: Les Binet and Peter Field.'

Within organizations it takes a cultural shift to move from being tactically focused and reactive to leading the strategic direction of the business. This comes with some internal pain as it may mean that you are suggesting changing the direction of the business and/or no longer focusing on areas of growth or choices the business made previously. It is also personally tough as it's easy to jump straight from opportunity to activation (this was a mistake I frequently made in my early strategic planning years). Instead, you need to take a step back and review the strategic options for how you will win against your competition in targeting and positioning and how you will best serve your customer's needs. But you've got this – let your insight (see *Chapter 7*) and commercial direction aid your decision-making.

APPROACHES TO MAKING STRATEGIC CHOICES

The traditional approach to strategic choices we have been taught for decades is known by the acronym STP: segmentation, targeting and positioning.

Once objectives have been set, an organization must decide on its strategy. This involves deciding how the organization might reach its objectives in terms of market and products. Part of this will involve making decisions around STP.

SEGMENTATION

Segmentation is the process of dividing a market up into smaller, more defined parts. These segments are usually formed as a result of defining the market by similar needs. This could be by industry, customers, audiences, interests, locations, size, etc.

TARGETING

Targeting as challenged by Byron Sharp

There is a school of thought from Byron Sharp of the Ehren-berg-Bass Institute for Marketing Science which challenges the traditional approach of STP. Sharp says that you don't need to target key customers within a category and that you can go after all the players in that category. According to this mode of thinking, your light buyers and those who haven't bought from you offer a greater commercial benefit than getting your existing buyers to use you more frequently.

Sharp, who is a professor of marketing sciences at the Ehrenberg-Bass Institute and author of the book *How Brands Grow*, uses rigorous scientific methodology across a number of categories and simplifies the principles of marketing down to seven core rules.[24] The key principles are that in order for our brand to be chosen by our customer, we need to have mental availability (being top of mind) and physical availability (being where customers shop).

How Brands Grow demonstrates that the brands which successfully grow (the ones with the highest market share) are the ones with universal appeal and the biggest customer base. This suggests that it makes more sense to advertise to everyone in the market for a product you sell rather than limit your communications to a small, segmented audience.

Sharp's seven rules for brand growth are as follows:

1. Continuously reach all buyers of the category, with both physical distribution and marketing communication
2. Be easy to buy
3. Get noticed
4. Refresh and build memory structures
5. Create distinctive communication assets
6. Be consistent yet fresh and interesting
7. Stay competitive and maintain mass appeal – don't give customers reasons not to buy your brand

Focus your efforts on the uncaring many – lots of light buyers who don't think about you, don't even buy you very often. So many of them are really important to your sales.

(Richard Bambrick, Global Senior Insight Lead, Pentland Brands)[25]

Tribal targeting

Tribal targeting is a psychological way of targeting. Instead of targeting by age, gender, demographics, geographical location and so on, it involves targeting based on beliefs and interests.

A tribe is a group of people who gather around a common mindset, set of goals, area of interest or shared passion. These people are travelling in the same direction, at the same speed. People subconsciously form tribes around nearly every interest niche you can think of, from cleaning 'Hinchers' (formed by Mrs Hinch, a relatable cleaning guru) to Marie Kondo's book *Spark Joy* (about decluttering).

One brand I have seen follow the tribal targeting approach is Tarquin's Cornish Gin, a premium gin brand created on the Cornish coast. Its brand positioning emphasizes its Cornish coast roots and helps it to tap into a close-knit tribe of surfers, aiming to become an aspirational brand for those wanting to be part of the surfing community. On a tactical level, Tarquin's branding can be found at beach bars and surfing competitions, with tasting boards shaped as surf boards.

The first step of using tribal targeting is to research and identify your tribe:

- Who is your audience?
- What are their interests?
- Where do they live online?

The second step is to find your tribe:

- What are they interested in?
- How do they interact with each other?

- Who are their influencers?
- Can you leverage existing tribes that have shared values and a common mindset with your brand?

The final step is to engage with your tribe:
- Ensure transparency of brand partnerships
- Create relevant and valuable content that appeals to the unique ties that bind the tribe
- Position your organization as a leader within that tribe
- Start a dialogue on the tribe's platforms and within their community
- Develop partnerships with influencers who can engage with the tribe on your behalf and provide endorsements

Influencers

The influencer strategy – a type of targeting – is worth mentioning in its own right. Here, an influencer either infiltrates an existing tribe that shares their values or uses their own tribe to promote and endorse products or services.

POSITIONING

Positioning determines how a product or service sits in the minds of customers versus the competition. This takes form as your brand positioning. To bring your brand to life, you will need to understand current and desired customer perceptions of your brand, position products through communication, and define and design an appropriate marketing mix.

Brand positioning

Brand positioning should be developed as part of the strategic process. Having defined the market opportunity, the segment in which you will operate, the target audience you will go after and the approach you will take, then and only then it is time to develop your brand positioning to leverage the opportunity. All positioning needs to be developed based on insight (which is discussed further in *Chapter 7*), while looking externally to the needs of your customers and the activities of your competitors. It should not be developed internally in isolation, with reference only to your organization's portfolio of brands. Yes, you may need to set your brands apart internally, but this should not be your only lens. Don't forget – a marketer's first job is always to ensure awareness of their brands.

All too often, I see brand positioning being developed outside of strategy. Almost the first thing many marketers do in a new role is to attempt to reposition and then redesign the brand – and then not too long after they resign. You should only touch the positioning or brand identity if one of the following four situations applies:

1. **There has been a change in market conditions**: If market conditions have significantly changed as a result of external factors (such as an increase in competition, new government legislation or wanting to target a new segment of the market), then repositioning and reinventing your brand will help you to remain current and competitive.

2. **You need to overcome negative brand associations**: Perhaps your customer's perceptions or brand associations are negative because of a failed product relaunch, poor communications or some other reason. Relaunching the brand will provide a clear line in the sand for customers, showing that your brand has changed and helping to create new brand associations. However, only do this once the internal issues that caused the bad reputation or negative brand association have been resolved. Without resolving the issues first, you won't change people's perceptions and will ultimately lose credibility.

3. **You need to attract new audiences or to drive a reappraisal among your existing or lapsed audience:** Perhaps your customer base is ageing or in decline, you are losing to your competition, or your customers are leaving the category and you therefore need to re-engage or target a new segment of the market. Rebranding can help you to attract a new target audience or to retain or gain lapsed users. It can ensure brand relevancy in light of customers' current and future needs.

4. **You need to enter a new market:** Perhaps your existing market is static and/or in decline and you therefore need to enter a new market or category to grow (maybe an adjacent category or a new market geographically). A rebrand may be necessary to increase your strength before entering a new market and/or to reflect the positioning of your brand in the new market with a different competitive set and customer needs.

Whatever your reasons for wanting to rebrand, remember that doing so always requires a strategic rationale for change.

A brand is more than just a logo, a visual identity or a set of guidelines (although all three are important). A brand is a promise of what you are going to enable consumers to do, think or feel. We all know a brand needs to be memorable (for all the right reasons). When built correctly, it will become an asset that will unlock the market and ensure business growth.

Brand positioning models

There are many different models you can use to capture the essence and positioning of your brand. I have seen everything from brand onions to brand keys to brand apples to brand Venn diagrams. You can use whatever you like, with one caveat. Your chosen method must allow you to capture your positioning based on customer insight, it must be externally focused (i.e. it must take account of your competition) and it must allow you to gain clarity on what sets you apart from your competition.

My personal favourite model is the brand pyramid. Why? Because it forces you to look externally to the market or category and to examine where you sit in relation to your competition. This stops you being internally focused. Populating this model always leads to a healthy level of tension between what you believe you offer as a point of difference and what may actually be the category norms (the points of parity). You may soon realize that there is not much that gives you a true sustainable point of difference (something you can safely own for three years or for the duration of your strategic timelines). *Figure 3.2* illustrates the brand pyramid.

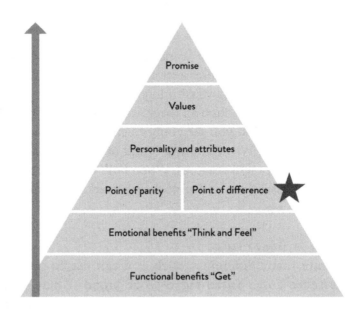

FIGURE 3.2 THE BRAND PYRAMID

Starting from the bottom, the brand pyramid considers the customer's perspective:

- What are you functionally going to provide (what will the customer 'get')?
- What are the emotional benefits (what will the customer 'think and feel')?

Then it looks to the market:

- Can your brand meet market expectations (point of parity)?
- What do you offer that your competitors don't (point of difference)?

Then it focuses back on the customer and the externally facing proposition:

- What makes your brand different in terms of its personality, point of view, attributes, etc.?
- What is significant about its values?
- What are you going to promise? (And can you deliver on it sustainably?)

The magic, though, is in the middle section. This is where you look at your competitive set (feel free to stretch your thinking here to include indirect competitors) and consider the following:

- **Points of parity**: These are attributes that are not unique to your brand and may be the same as attributes of other brands. They are elements you need to have to be able to credibly operate in your category or market and where you need to at least match your competition.
- **Points of difference**: These are attributes or benefits that are only offered by your brand. They differentiate you and may also allow you to be seen as superior to other brands in your category or market.

Protecting your brand

Once you have spent time developing, testing and aligning your brand internally and externally, it is important to define how you can ensure you protect both your brand positioning and (when externally facing) your brand identity. It is vital to develop and capture your brand to provide clarity for all stakeholders and to ensure that the positioning forms the basis of:

- **Communication and identity**: consistency at every single touchpoint
- **Communication decisions**: what you say and how you say it
- **Clarity to develop**: propositions and innovation against brand positioning

Chapter 5 will discuss in more detail what customers are looking for from brands today. However, for now, remember that they are looking for brands that reflect their aspirations in life, so you need to communicate not what you do but why you do it. Especially in Britain, customers want brands that are transparent, ethical and sustainable, and they love to support the underdog (i.e. the challenger brand).

THE LONG AND THE SHORT OF IT: LES BINET AND PETER FIELD

Some of you might have been reading this chapter thinking, "That's great strategically, but I also need to tactically deliver and gain commercial growth in the short term." I hear you. In this chapter, I am just going to point you to the thinking of Les Binet and Peter Field of the Institute of Practitioners in Advertising. They are the kings of advertising and marketing effectiveness. In their *The Long and the*

Short of It, they have proven that we need a combination of strategic (long-term) brand-building activities and tactics (the short game) to deliver sales in the here and now and thereby sustainably grow.[26] *Chapter 4* looks further at how to bring these plans to life tactically.

WHAT GOOD LOOKS LIKE

- Strategic choices have been made that deliver against the organization's vision, mission and desired legacy
- The strategy will deliver the organization's commercial growth aspirations and is of an appropriate size
- The strategy can be validated with insight
- Targeting choices have been made
- Positioning has been developed

WHAT BAD LOOKS LIKE

- Choices are not made: the organization goes after every market opportunity and spreads its resources and energy too thinly, and so does not make an impact against its competition
- There is a lack of understanding of the distinction between strategy and tactical focus (it is a combination of the two that is the winning formula)
- A strategy has been written but is not followed

QUESTIONS TO ASK YOURSELF

- Are you clear on your organization's wider vision, mission and commercial objectives?
- Are you able to identify which markets you should continue to operate in, exit and enter?
- Are you truly able to set SMART objectives and support your team to do so?

- Are your objectives interlinked and is there a commercial thread running through them?
- Are you able to make a choice about how to target your customer?
- Are you able to develop positioning that is based on external market opportunities, that sets you apart from the competition based on true customer insight and that has a sustainable point of difference?
- Are you able to capture this positioning and act as a guardian, ensuring that your brand positioning is understood and consistently communicated?

CAPTURE TIME: KEY DISCOVERIES

1.

2.

3.

WHAT THREE THINGS ARE YOU GOING TO DO TO IMPROVE?

1.

2.

3.

CHAPTER SUMMARY

In this chapter we looked at the elements involved in making strategic choices to allow you to meet your objectives and deliver on your organization's vision and mission. We examined differing approaches to STP and the importance of making a choice (even if it is to target all customers) so as to provide focus, direction and enhanced commercial impact. These factors, however, are all part of the long game. In the next chapter we will look at how to bring your strategy to life in your annual plans, mixing activities to deliver the strategy but also gain short-term commercial success.

CHAPTER 4

BRING THE STRATEGY TO LIFE THROUGH ANNUAL PLANS AND TACTICS

In this chapter we will build on the strategic objectives and goals discussed in *Chapter 3* by examining annual plans, which serve to bring the strategy to life through tactics. We will also look at changes in the marketing mix, the importance of using the full and latest marketing mix, and how to deliver these in an omnichannel approach to meet and exceed customers' ever-growing expectations and changing behaviour.

TRANSLATING STRATEGY INTO ANNUAL PLANS

Having set your three- to five-year strategy and commercial goals, you now need to define what the next year (or 18 months) of this strategy will look like in practice and, if possible, drill down into what will happen in each quarter. Planning out your annual calendar is often part of the strategic planning process. It's used to show that your strategic objectives are actionable and also that you have planned how and when you will deliver your tactics in the market. *Figure 4.1* shows an example format for an annual plan split up into quarters.

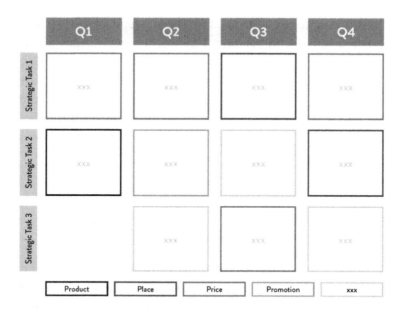

FIGURE 4.1 AN EXAMPLE ANNUAL PLAN

Having this level of clarity on what will happen will both reflect and inform your forecasting and commercial data. It will also provide clarity when you are briefing your agency partners or other functions on the KPIs and commercial deliverables for each of the planned activities.

Agile marketing (see *Chapter 2*) is both a strategic and a tactical approach. If you plan to adopt this approach, you may want to create annual, quarterly, monthly or fortnightly objectives and key results (OKRs) that feed into your annual or long-term vision. You can then work in two-week bursts to test, deliver, learn and evolve.

TOP TIPS FOR 'FROM AND TO' STATEMENTS

Break down the 'from and to' statements (see *Chapter 2*) from your long-term strategy into annual goals. For example:

	Long term		Annual	
	From	To	From	To
TURNOVER	£1.8 million	£3.6 million	£1.8 million	£2.3 million
MARKET SHARE VALUE	3%	6%	3%	4%
PROFIT TRADING CONTRIBUTION	23%	26%	23%	23.5%
PENETRATION	1%	3%	1%	1.5%

SHARE TIME

Too often, I see annual or strategic objectives stated on the brief to an agency or on the internal timeline for a single campaign. By all means share these high-level objectives, but also share the specific roles and objectives the campaign or activation needs to deliver. Take the annual targets and break them down to give campaign specifics.

THE MARKETING MIX OF TODAY

The full marketing mix comprises everything us marketers have in our armoury to bring our plans to life. It is commonly considered to be made up of the 7 Ps: product, place, price, promotion, people, process and physical evidence. We should really concern ourselves with all seven, regardless of whether we are offering a product or service, as we now live in an experience economy.

Table 4.1 shows examples of the 7 Ps in today's landscape.

PRODUCT	Quality
	Features and benefits
	User experience
	Variants, mix and range
	Branding, packaging, format and pack design
	Support
	Customer service
	Availability and warranties
PLACE	*Direct to consumer:*
	Online, mobile, owned outlet, salesperson or app
	Indirect:
	In-store, outlets, online
	On or off trade
	Third party:
	Wholesale, distributor, trade channels or franchise
PRICE	Positioning
	Total cost (variable + fixed costs)
	Portfolio play:
	Loss leaders, market skimming and market penetration
	Customer led
	Price elasticity
	Discounts:
	Performance, rebates and payment terms
	Value added, percentage off, money-back guarantees
	Sales promotions
	Subscription memberships

PROMOTION	Advertising, e.g. TV, print, cinema, outdoor and radio
	Digital marketing, e.g. pay-per-click and search engine optimization
	Social media (paid, earned and owned)
	Public relations
	Direct marketing
	Branding
	Promotional marketing
	Sales promotion
	Experiential
	Corporate social responsibility
	Sponsorship
	Shopper/Trade marketing
PEOPLE	Customer-facing staff
	Sales advisers in outlets
	Customer service, e.g. chatbots
	Brand ambassadors
	Trade channels
	Sales support
	Culture and image
	Training and skills
	Remuneration
PROCESS	Focus on customer experience
	Online and offline user experience
	Fulfilment
	Customer relationship post-purchase
PHYSICAL EVIDENCE	Sales staff contact and their presentation
	Tangible items, e.g. chairs, collateral and tickets
	Experience of the brand
	Online expertise

TABLE 4.1 THE MODERN MARKETING MIX

Since the 7 Ps were developed, many more activation platforms have become available. The digital age has created much new technology, in which we are immersed on a day-to-day basis, but for me these new technologies still sit within the 7 Ps. Daniel Rowles of Target Internet says:

> Digital is not this separate thing – it's just part of marketing and all the key principles still apply. It's a set of channels we're using. However, digital has strategically changed everything – how we communicate with one another, how we buy and research things. So, I would actually see it more as a fast-changing environment that affects everything else.
>
> (Daniel Rowles, CEO, Target Internet)[27]

As a result of these changes, there has been an evolution in the marketing mix, with alternative conceptions to the 7 Ps emerging. *Table 4.2* shows how there has been a move from a functional to an emotion-based experience (note that the 4 Ps are the original items in the 7 Ps, to which the other three were later added).

4 Ps	4 Cs	4 Es
Product	Customer	Experience
Place	Convenience	Everywhere
Price	Cost	Exchange
Promotion	Communication	Evangelism

TABLE 4.2 EVOLUTION IN THE MARKETING MIX

TOP TIPS FOR IMPLEMENTING
THE MARKETING MIX

Whichever combination you use – the Ps, Cs or Es – ensure you consider them all. During the strategic planning process, people too often jump from market or customer opportunity to tactics, not only missing out the strategic planning stage but also usually only focusing on a new or existing product's launch and/or new promotions. You have so much more in your armoury to enable you not only to engage with your customers but also to outperform your competition.

KEY ASPECTS OF
THE MARKETING MIX

Certain marketing mix activities are particularly being focused on by the industry today.

DIGITAL AND SOCIAL MEDIA

Digital and social media sit within promotion, and online and ecommerce activities sit within place or promotion.

I have no doubt that additional activation methods will arise, and some may cease to be used, but our role as marketers is to keep abreast of these changes, select those that are more relevant to our customers, use them as part of an omnichannel approach, and test and learn.

There has been an increased demand on marketers to use social media platforms to communicate because these platforms are both economical and measurable. They can also be used to deliver a form of insight. However, whether social media is paid (display ads, reach), owned (your brand social media platforms) or earned (shared by your community or wider, influencers), it won't always be the most relevant platform for your target audience or customers. Selecting the right platforms for your target audience is key, as is appreciating that you need to do more than just dump your message and run. These platforms need interaction and engagement with communities. Social media is also the most influential channel in the decision-making process, so it should not be ignored.

> Social media is an opportunity to really connect and communicate with audiences – not talking at them, but listening and learning what's going on, conversing with them in a very human way, really engaging so that you can build brand relationships and engagement.
>
> In fact, the number one influencing channel is social media. We will go there – we will look to what others are doing, we will trust in what others are doing and we will engage. It's almost like the 'wisdom of the crowd' concept. So, from a consumer perspective, we now trust these channels far more than we ever did before.
>
> **(Michelle Carvill, Director, Carvill Creative)**[28]

DIGITAL MARKETING

Digital marketing is the use of digital platforms, the internet and technology to reach, engage and interact with customers. Target Internet periodically conducts digital skills benchmarks in which they test 5,000 marketers on their actual skills, not just their opinions. In this way, they identify skill gaps across the board. Daniel Rowles of Target Internet, when reviewing the findings, stated the following:

> It's appalling – there is a massive skills gap. The more junior people have improved. We did [the benchmark test] back in 2018 and we've just done it again now [in 2020]. And there is some really good improvement at graduate and intern level and up to executive level, but at head-of-department level it's gone backwards.
>
> What's happening is the environment is moving so quickly that users' expectations are changing. Users expect your website to be better, your app to be better, and the customer service interactions to be better and more digitally joined up. Therefore, if my skills as a department kind of stay the same, even if I've got no responsibility for actually implementing this stuff, I don't know the right questions to ask.
>
> I don't know how to challenge my agency, and I don't know why and what I should be measuring, because the environment is moving so quickly around me. What this means is that if your skills aren't constantly being updated, you are basically getting left behind step by step.
>
> It's moving so quickly that if you did learn about something a couple of years ago and you've not updated your knowledge, you're going backwards.
>
> (Daniel Rowles, CEO, Target Internet)[29]

The message is clear: our marketing landscape is constantly evolving and technological developments are being made at such a rapid pace. We need to continually invest in ourselves, through training, to learn the changes in technology to ensure that our experience is reflective of consumer or customers' expectations.

CHALLENGER BRANDS

There has been a rise in challenger brands, which are brands and start-ups that have identified a customer need that is not being satisfied by a category. This often results in disruption to category norms.

This is possible because the barriers to entering established markets have been reduced. Historically, businesses needed capital, significant marketing investment, and established size and scale to enter a market. However, due to digital communications providing a lower-cost way to communicate en masse, retailers' expectations have been lessened and they now commonly support challenger brands. Additionally, options such as crowdfunding to raise investment have made entering new markets far more achievable. Another factor is that once they have entered, they don't necessarily have to deal with complex infrastructures or processes, so they are able to flex and bring products and services to market with speed.

There has also been a rise of challenger brands serving the market directly through subscription offerings. They offer ease, convenience, personalization and often a saving, and in this way they have substituted more traditional routes to market. Examples include Bloom & Wild, Pasta Evangelists and Tails.com.

WHAT IS FUELLING THIS FOCUS?

In the ever-changing marketing mix landscape,[30] three key factors are fuelling the industry's focus:

- **Economic pressures**: the need to do more with less
- **Technological demands**: the need to stay up to speed
- **High customer expectations**: brand purpose and changing customer demand

Some further factors are explored in the following sections.

CUSTOMER BUYING POWER

As customers' buying power and choices have increased, with a better understanding of what they want, their expectations have shifted. They are no longer simply looking for a functional transaction to acquire a product at a certain price in a convenient location, having seen the product in a campaign (where emotional benefits were added in). They are looking for an experience that they can access whenever and wherever they want (usually instantly and digitally), where there is an exchange beyond gaining the product for money. They want to become part of a brand or community, and the experience should be so emotionally fuelled and positive that they share it verbally and digitally with their tribe and peers.

If you build your brand connection by enhancing the human connection with your existing and future customers, they will become raving fans who want to come back to you time and time again.

The experience economy is the next thing up from the service economy. If you're just focusing on the ROI of an individual experiential activation, you're not really thinking about the customer experience as a whole entity, in relation to all the touchpoints with your brand. If the customer goes and buys your product or service online afterwards, then that should not be a problem for you and you shouldn't be scared of it. You should be embracing that.

Stop thinking about brand activations as a kind of separate tag-on that you pass on to your PR agency to organize. Instead, make it the very heart of your strategy and think about all the additional benefits, such as gaining insight and being able to directly communicate with your customer. Start to think about the experience at the very start of any kind of marketing strategy.

(Meredith O'Shaughnessy, CEO and Wizard, Meredith Collective)[31]

BETTER UNDERSTANDING OF WHAT CUSTOMERS WANT

Our understanding of what customers want from brands and businesses has improved. We have more data – and in turn insight – to inform what products and services we offer and how we do so. We have also, as an industry, improved our understanding of how customers truly behave and make decisions. *Chapter 7* covers this in more depth, looking at behavioural science and particularly System 1 and System 2 thinking.

SHIFTS IN CONSUMER EXPECTATIONS

Consumers now hold more power. There has been an increase in competition for us as marketers, but this means more choice and power for them. They no longer need to settle and have realized their voice not only counts but is king.

Consumers are also not restricted by location, with distribution and technological advances meaning they can access products and services anywhere. They have always held the power of recommendation or evangelism, but in the digital age their voice can reach many people instantly – with positive or negative results for a brand.

With an increase in consumerism, many have turned to experiences over material items, leading to the rise of the experience economy.

The result is that marketing is no longer just about communicating to consumers what your product or service is about. You have to let them know what experience it will deliver.

THE NEED FOR INNOVATION

Innovation is still an important aspect of the product and service offering. We still need to make shifts in our profession in only naming truly innovative products as innovative (new and disruptive) products and services. Additionally, innovation (not existing product development) should be based on customer insight, especially as customers have a high level of expectation around innovation, particularly concerning experiences.

There are lots of theories on how to grow brands, but I genuinely feel that a way to bring your focus or strategy to life is through innovation, because that's how consumers experience it.

(Shweta Harit, Global Vice President of Marketing, Evian)[32]

The technical skill of innovation involves many of the abilities covered throughout this book, namely:

- The ability to develop and use insight and your deep-rooted understanding of your customers to identify a need or a gain or a pain point
- The ability to deliver on or solve this pain or gain point creatively, and the ability to ideate (see next section) a concept, a solution or propositions
- The ability to use commercial acumen to identify commercial benefits and gain resources from business customers

- The ability to use data collection to select the most relevant concepts, engage in product testing and seek feedback from customers
- The ability to tell stories to retailers and customers to convey a need and its solution
- A can-do attitude and resilience

In addition, you will need to have a strong understanding of:
- Product portfolio matrix management (e.g. the Ansoff and Boston Consulting Group's matrix models (Boston Consulting Group 1968))
- Technical or product development and gate process (either an understanding of your organization's existing processes or the ability to create and establish new processes to move a product from idea to launch)
- Project management skills to enable you to lead cross-functional teams, meet check-off points and work within required timings
- How to translate concepts into customer-facing entities (e.g. pack design, service propositions, communications and support plans)

DESIGN THINKING

Design thinking is rising in popularity as a new way of coming up with solutions to problems and creating innovative digital products. It is fast paced and iterative, and it looks to understand users, challenge assumptions, redefine problems, and create innovative solutions to prototype and test. It has five phases: empathize, define, ideate, prototype and test. It is most useful in tackling pain or gain points that are unknown or have not yet been identified.

METHODS OF COMMUNICATION

The increase in digital communications has resulted in a reduction of face-to-face interaction and an increase in the activities around online communities and tribes. Customers are also looking for your brand or business to reflect the aspirational life they want to live or be part of. When their needs are satisfied, they feel connected to your business, community and tribe.

Additionally, people expect brands and businesses to be transparent in what they promise and what they do. Relatedly, people now have more ready access to information, and they are often quick to use this information to uncover, name and shame brands that are not perceived to be acting ethically.

It is also worth remembering that this increased digital media consumption has not replaced traditional media but added to the amount of media we consume. It is more difficult to cut through the 'noise' as there has been an increase in the number of messages customers see daily, and attention has been reduced due to dual screening; the use of two screens at once.

> You watch TV in a different way now – you sit there with your device, you look at print or you're walking around with these devices attached to you the whole time. This has changed the way that humans interact with the world around them.
>
> (Daniel Rowles, CEO, Target Internet)[33]

THE OMNICHANNEL APPROACH

Marketing has for some time now focused its energies on developing integrated marketing communications, which move customers through decision-making or buying behaviour journeys.

The AIDA model (awareness, interest, desire and action)[34] is commonly used to map this process. Historically, moving a customer from awareness to action took two weeks from above the line (ATL) to through the line (TTL) and below the line (BTL) as they moved from an advert they had seen to purchasing in an outlet. But with end-to-end platforms like Instagram, which have a shop function contained within the app, we can move customers from awareness to action in less than a minute. For example, I recently took 19 seconds to move from an Instagram ad to purchase (a pair of pink striped pyjamas in case you are wondering!).

We have moved from multi-channel, where the same message is deployed on multiple communications platforms, to omnichannel, where the message is tailored depending on where in the decision-making pathway the customer is. We can do this due to the increased insight we now have.

The term 'omnichannel' marketing (from 'omni,' meaning 'in all ways or places') therefore refers to the concept of providing a seamless user experience across all channels relevant to the customer's journey.

The key focus here is the customer's journey. The way a customer progresses through platforms and seeks or uses information is no longer linear and now combines both online and offline modes (all technically forms of 'promotion'). The way in which customers move through the process will differ – you may have multiple customers' journeys to consider, and it may be that no two are the same. Insight therefore is key to understanding not only a customer's journey but also what they need to see, hear and feel at each stage to enable them to progress. This will allow you to tailor your messaging and decide on the right platforms to use. *Figure 4.2* illustrates how a customer's journey might pass through multiple platforms.

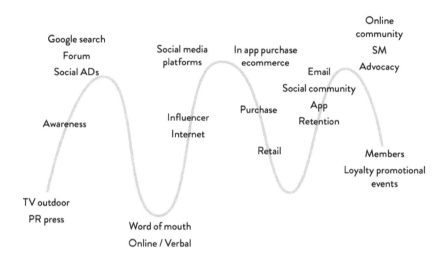

FIGURE 4.2 OMNICHANNEL: A CUSTOMER'S JOURNEY

So how do we cut through the noise? What must our marketing messages do and say? *Chapter 7* will look at this topic further, examining the role System 1 thinking has and exploring the advantages emotional messaging has over functional messaging. This knowledge can be used to create an effective piece of communication or advertising that resonates with customers.

As a marketer, never claim you own the customer experience because you don't ... The customer experience is the result of everything the company does.

In fact, by claiming you own it, measuring it and then telling people it's your job to make it better, you're setting yourself up for a very big failure because you can never deliver that. My advice is to find a way to tell everybody else how they're doing, do it consistently and put yourself into a position of power.

(Thomas Barta, Founder, The Marketing Leadership Masterclass)[35]

WHAT GOOD LOOKS LIKE

- Annual SMART objectives exist (see *Chapter 3*) with clarity on what needs to be done both qualitatively and quantitatively, including in commercial terms
- How this will be achieved has been outlined on a quarterly basis with reference to the various mix activities
- The full marketing mix (not just product or promotion) has been considered and/or is being used to bring the plans to life
- Customers' increasing expectations are met or exceeded
- You are truly being led by insight into your customers' journey and appreciation of all the platforms they visit to ensure that you are not only meeting them where they are but also tailoring your messages to what they need to hear at each point in the process
- You are using increased understanding of your customers' behaviour in your messaging

WHAT BAD LOOKS LIKE

- You are using linear, planned campaigns that don't correlate with the customer's buying journey
- You are expecting customers to come to you, but the competition is too strong to justify this – you are asking

customers to work too hard without giving them an experience that makes it worth their time

- Your plans focus only on communications or existing product development
- There is a lack of appreciation of the speed with which we all now operate and the nature of the digital environment

---

QUESTIONS TO ASK YOURSELF

- Have you set your annual objectives based on your long-term strategy? Have you shared and modelled them within your forecasting and commercial data? Do you have suitable linked KPIs?
- Have you defined the role that your planned mix activities or campaigns will deliver to contribute to this annual and/or strategic movement?
- Are you using or at least considering the full marketing mix (any or all of the types) to bring your strategic plans to life?
- Are you aware of how your customers' expectations have changed or increased? What are your plans to close any gaps between those expectations and what is actually happening?
- Are you aware of how your customers are currently consuming media? What are the most relevant platforms?
- Are you mapping and delivering truly insight-based integrative communications using an omnichannel approach? What insight do you need to allow you to make this shift?
- Are there any new platforms you want to test and learn?
- How do you set KPIs and measure process for each element of the activation or mix activity that you put into the market?
- How do you use this information not only to improve your effectiveness but also as a form of insight?
  - › **Products and services:** Does your current product or service portfolio meet or exceed customers' expectations? How can you develop your products or services to meet,

exceed or enhance the experience and meet market and customer opportunities? Based on customer insight, what are the pain and gain points?

> **Price:** Do you need to review your pricing structure? Does it reflect the exchange customers expect?

> **Place and access:** What new distribution options are there for customers to experience and access your product (online, in-store experience, mobile, etc.)?

> **Promotion:** Are you using the best promotional and communication channels with the right messages, at the right places, at the right times, using an omnichannel approach?

- What is your and your team's understanding of digital marketing, social media and ecommerce, skill gaps and areas of focus?

> **Physical evidence:** What tangible items are your customers interacting with? Do they reflect and enhance your desired brand experience?

> **People:** Which of your people are your customers interacting and engaging with? Are these people appropriately skilled and delivering the correct brand experience? Are there any skill gaps you need to close?

> **Process:** Does the way in which your customers receive or experience your products or services meet and exceed their expectations? Does it deliver an experience?

CAPTURE TIME: KEY DISCOVERIES

1.

2.

3.

WHAT THREE THINGS ARE YOU
GOING TO DO TO IMPROVE?

1.

2.

3.

CHAPTER SUMMARY

In this chapter, we looked at how to translate strategies into annual goals and plans, ensuring you are using the full and latest marketing mix and customer insight to build innovative forms of communication based on what customers want and need. In the next chapter we will look at how to work with agency partners to bring these plans to life to deliver your objectives.

CHAPTER 5

WORKING WITH AGENCY PARTNERS

In this chapter we will focus on the essential role of a key stakeholder: activation agencies, whether internal or external. These play a crucial role in bringing plans to life and in developing and delivering impactful yet commercially effective activation. Agencies can also help in delivering the long- and short-term strategic plan and other marketing objectives, and ultimately delivering the commercial agenda while also developing and delivering brand messaging and communications that disrupt, engage and drive the desired customer movement. Not a lot to ask, eh?

You may be reading this thinking, "I know how to manage agencies and brief them to deliver campaigns that drive the required customer movement and are commercially effective." If that's the case, then I ask you to bring a beginner's mind to this chapter and engage with it as a refresher or 'audit,' to double check and ensure you are still doing these things or check that the team you manage is doing so.

The aim of this chapter is to reframe your thinking about what an agency relationship could and should look like. This should help you to create optimum working relationships and outputs, and move your agency relationships from service contracts to partnerships. 'Agency partner' is a term I coined to reflect the required shift in this relationship.

If I am honest, in my earlier career, I used agencies as a service. However, through experiencing the benefits of building partnerships with agencies and seeing them as an extension of the team, and through my work today sitting on both sides of the fence, I have learned that the most fruitful relationship is a partnership that ensures both parties are equal. This is where the magic happens.

I have a personal passion to improve the agency–client relationship. I help to improve this working relationship by training client-side marketers via my Chartered Institute of Marketing course on agency briefing and management and in-house courses, and by training agency-side marketers in-house or via an Institute of Promotional Marketing and AAR diploma on how to become a strategic partner with commercial acumen.

There is potentially scope for a whole other book on this topic alone, so this chapter builds on my experience to give you the major points for consideration.

THE IMPORTANCE OF HIGH-QUALITY AGENCY–CLIENT RELATIONSHIPS

As explained in *Chapter 1*, marketers' roles have expanded but time is limited, and we can no longer focus purely on communications. We therefore need a partner who has a full understanding of our brand and business, our current position, and where we are going in the short and long term. With this clarity, they will be able to exercise more autonomy in their delivery and take up less of our time – of which we simply don't have enough.

In addition, with our increased commercial responsibility, we need to demonstrate both short-term and long-term ROI in marketing and show that we are achieving against KPIs. This is for both in-house (increasingly content and design are being brought in-house) and external agency partners. So, our agency partners need to have the necessary commercial understanding and visibility to be aligned with our commercial goals and targets.

KEY ELEMENTS IN AN AGENCY PARTNERSHIP

An excellent agency–client partnership requires the following elements.

TRANSPARENCY

Having taken the time to set out your long-term strategy, your strategic approach, your annual marketing plans and then your campaign objectives, you will need to share these with your agency partner (and in fact, in an ideal world, your agency partner will have been involved in this process). This is so your agency partner feels aligned with your goals (as they say, 'one team, one dream'); understands the dependencies between your vision, corporate objectives, strategy, marketing objectives and campaign activities; and understands their role in delivering all of this.

And, as you will be striving to deliver the same commercial goal, all commercial data and performance data also need to be shared (if there are any objections, they should be nothing a non-disclosure agreement won't solve). Finally, details of any internal changes or challenges that may arise should also be shared.

BEING AN EXTENSION OF THE CLIENT TEAM

Treat your agency partner as you would anyone else in your internal team. Agencies are not there to serve us but work with us, as one team, to deliver the same objectives. They should ideally function as an extension of your team, with each party respecting the other's skill set and process.

TOP TIPS FOR INITIATIVES TO HELP YOU WORK WITH AN AGENCY AS A TEAM

- **Induction:** make this the same as you would give to anyone in your team
- **Transparency and visibility:** share the same commercial data and performance data as you would with your team
- **Define ways of working from the offset:** these include but are not limited to:
  - > Preferred method of contact
  - > Frequency of meetings and contact location
  - > Learning styles
  - > Values (see more information on defining values in *Unit 3*)
- **Space for co-working:** even if it is done remotely
- **Collaboration and involvement:** encourage these at all key meetings to develop long-term strategies, brand positioning, creative platforms, etc. (at the very least, ensure there is a debrief on all thinking arising from the meeting)

Marketing is all about effectiveness and this tenet extends to the client–agency relationship also. It should come as no surprise, but the most successful campaigns and projects are those where agency personnel truly feel like integrated members of a dedicated 'project team.' Effectiveness also refers to process. When they are well prepared and well run, workshops can not only foster closer, more productive client–agency relationships; they can also generate effectiveness of output. Of course, there are times when agency and client stakeholders will need to go off and work or review independently. But working together as skilled professionals can help you identify approaches, spark discussion and align on key principles in the moment, rather than waiting a week for a 'big reveal' in a presentation.

Some of the most enjoyable working sessions I have had in my career have been working with clients in a room with Post-it notes on the wall, snacks on the table and fire in the belly of everyone seeing the solutions materialize in front of them, as one team. Agency life can be tough, demanding and full on, but agency professionals care deeply and passionately about the projects and brands that they work on. Helping to facilitate more integrated client–agency 'teams' and relationships not only makes for more effective working relationships but more effective marketing output: something welcomed by all parties.

(Callum Saunders, Head of Planning, Zeal Creative)[36]

RESPECT FOR THE DISCIPLINE AND SKILL SET

Agency partners are skilled at creatively project managing the delivery of activation into the market and translating marketers' briefs into engaging and disruptive messages and ideas. In doing so, they help to deliver the desired customer behaviour change, keeping on brand while delivering the KPIs.

Marketers' roles, as guardians, is to ensure that any creative platform or idea presented is on brand, will deliver the desired customer movement, and will deliver against the required KPIs and ROI. It is not our role to dictate or shorten the creative course, stunt the process and thereby limit the success of the outputs.

With regard to feedback, as mentioned you are of course the brand guardian. However, before you begin making suggestions about making the logo bigger or have a go at rewriting the copy, do pause to remember that many agency personnel are highly qualified in their specific skill set (such as copywriting or graphic communication design) and may have a raft of professional qualifications and years of experience. It will always be more appreciated if you explain to the agency how the work does not meet the brief or is not on brand, rather than recreating for them your own version in a PowerPoint, however tempting that is.

UNDERSTANDING OF THE CREATIVE AND RESPONDING PROCESS

You must give your agency partners adequate time to effectively respond to your brief and requests. Agencies usually ask for a minimum of two weeks for a reason. Do you understand the process? If not, ask what their process is.

I would suggest allowing a minimum of three weeks for agencies to respond to a full brief and/or give you a pitch. Of course, artwork amends do not need to follow the same flow, so ask your agency for timings based on their process for your brand, as these will depend on the remuneration and contract.

Figure 5.1 shows the process that an agency is likely to follow in the two or three weeks they spend digesting your brief.

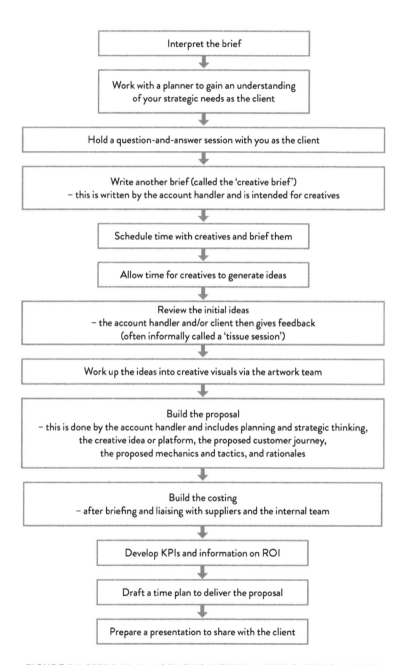

FIGURE 5.1 STEPS IN AN AGENCY'S INTERNAL RESPONSE TO A BRIEF

It is clear from *Figure 5.1* why agencies need a minimum of two weeks, and I would often suggest three or four for a pitch as they will need time to get under the skin of you as an organization and schedule time with all the necessary departments in the agency (which may already be booked). I appreciate that coming to the decision to appoint a new agency can itself be a daunting task, and so is requesting a pitch; this is why I help so many client-side marketers with pitch management.

Also bear in mind that for the agency it's a very intense, demanding and stressful process, in many cases with no remuneration. There is excitement about getting a crack at a great new product, brand or client, but there is also time pressure and a lot riding on the outcome. Do be respectful throughout the process, not culling agencies a few days before pitch day or adding excessively to the brief ahead of pitch day.

Regardless of the outcome, always provide thorough and constructive feedback to all agencies you have included in your pitch, almost as a thank you for their efforts. It can be useful to develop a scorecard to help you assess each agency against your criteria. This scorecard will outline the key criteria you are looking for in your future agency partner, and should be weighted to reflect the importance of each of these criteria and allow you to capture both numerical scores and comments. You can then ask each of your team members attending the pitch to use the scorecard to capture feedback. This will allow you to provide consolidated feedback and make it less likely that, as time passes, you will let this important step slide.

BRIEFING

I was once training a well-known retailer's marketing team on the importance of briefing. At the start, the senior marketer introducing the session stood up and said, "Guys, 'crap in, crap out,' so take the time to listen and learn how we can get better." That has stuck with me. In my experience, there are four elements to briefing: writing, alignment, delivery and refinement.

SHARE TIME

I see many briefs, both when I am helping agencies to respond more strategically to their clients' briefs and when I am supporting client-side marketers to find the right partner by inviting pitches or improving their briefing skills. I would say nine times out of ten, I can accurately guess the level of marketer who wrote the brief from its quality and the information provided. Non-SMART objectives (see *Chapter 3*), a lack of strategic context and explanations of past campaigns usually mean a more junior author. Strategic and wider organizational context, insight and required KPIs generally point to a more senior author.

WRITING A BRIEF

A well-written brief should take you all day to create – and it should not be given verbally over the phone or toplined in an email. The process of writing will force you to ensure you have considered all elements and that you have provided focus and clarity.

Briefs should be structured from the outside (market and trends) in and look to give context; home in on the challenge; provide clarity on the movement required, the brand, the customer and commercial factors; and define success and/or the deliverables.

Following is a suggested outline structure for a brief:

1. **Project details**
   › Basic facts: company, brand, product, project, author, client team, agency team, date and purchase order (yours will not be the only brief coming into the agency and there may even be multiple briefs from your brand or business – a purchase order shows commitment and organizational alignment)

2. **Background**
   › Starting point: where you are now, what you want to change and what you are already doing to change it
   › External background: market, competition and customers
   › Internal background: company, brand and product
   › Key issues facing the brand, product and communications, and hence the strategy

3. **Communication role and objectives**
   › 'From and to' movement (see *Chapter 2*): where are you now, where do you want to get to and how are you going to get there?
   › Communication strategy: pathway to the future and alignment of media (agencies) to achieve the goal
   › Single, measurable communication objective: e.g. improvement in sales, usage, awareness, image, reputation or response

4. **Target audience**
   › Rich, vivid descriptions: Who are they? What are their needs? What is their usage of the product? What is their relationship with the brand? What are their attitudes and values?
   › What do they think, feel and do now and what do you want them to think, feel and do in the future?

› The results of any relevant qualitative and quantitative research

› Proposition (crucial to the success of a brief)

› The single most compelling and competitive reason for customers to choose the company, brand or product

5. **Insight and data**
   › The proof or evidence you offer to support your claim
   › Evidence to substantiate why you are better than the competition

6. **Desired response or results**
   › What would success and failure look like?
   › Share past KPIs and ROI figures (see *Chapter 6*) to share learnings and allow realistic yet stretching targets to be set
   › The measure of success: What will be measured? How will it be measured? Who will measure it? What budget will be set aside to measure it?

7. **Creative guidelines and tone of voice**
   › Brand guidelines, personality and tone of voice affecting communication
   › If you would like mock-up creative visuals as part of the response, you will need to provide assets, pack shots and a copy of your brand guidelines along with your brief

8. **Mandatory requirements**
   › Media strategy and requirements
   › Budget
   › Timings
   › Legal and regulatory requirements
   › Any other information specific to your organization or product

9. **Approvals**
   > Who has authority?
   > Who is responsible, accountable, consulted and informed (RACI)?

GETTING ALIGNMENT ON A BRIEF

Having written the brief, have a colleague who is not close to the brand read it and provide suggestions and feedback. Give the opportunity to those in the RACI to review and provide suggestions. Only then should you share the brief with the agency.

The brief should be completed in full. Of course, as time goes on and you enter into a partnership way of working with an agency, the level of detail in the background context may only need to be given in summary form or as an appendix, but it should not be forgotten. This reduced need for background context is a benefit of a developed relationship and of providing a full understanding of your business and its history via your induction and work to date.

DELIVERY OF THE BRIEF

It should also be delivered face to face/virtually with a goal to inspire the agency partner about the challenge and opportunity the brief provides. If you are not motivated, why should they be? Where could you go to deliver this brief? Could you do it in the location that is reflective of your challenge; in the retail outlet, train, office building, store, home of where the activation needs to take place or where the customers are?

REFINEMENT OF THE BRIEF

Having shared the brief with your agency partner, you will need to update it to incorporate any suggestions they provide and to reflect any questions they have asked. It can then be locked down. Ensure the final brief is recirculated as this will become the definitive version against which proposals are measured. If you don't do this, giving constructive feedback becomes very difficult as there is no formalization of your needs and requirements to refer back to. There is a risk you will end up judging proposals against what you asked for (verbally) and what you feel, rather than a clearly documented set of criteria.

AGENCY MANAGEMENT
REGULAR PERFORMANCE REVIEWS

It is important to regularly review the performance of both parties. Key success measures for each function should be set at the beginning of the relationship and each subsequent year, and agreed together. These measures can act like personal development plans, which can run alongside the campaign objectives.

When client-side marketing teams come to me asking for help in soliciting pitches to find a new agency, its often because their agency is no longer delivering creatively, no longer bringing new thinking or not offering new ways of working. Relationships may have disintegrated, and the agency may no longer be aligned with where the client is strategically taking the brand. The majority of these are areas that could have been covered in a review and then addressed.

Do allow your agency partners the opportunity to periodically receive open feedback and give them time to make adjustments. Also, if you do decide to re-pitch or reappoint, then it is less of a shock and makes it more likely you will part on good terms.

REMUNERATION

The key point here is that remuneration should reflect the relationship you need to have. If you require immediate responsiveness, you will need to remunerate your agency with a monthly retainer. If you are doing projects periodically, then project-by-project fees may be suitable.

You can also remunerate agencies in the following ways:

- Commission
- Rate card multiplied by number of hours
- Fixed or phased fee
- Payment by results
- Minimum income guarantee
- Bonus

Finally, bear in mind that unless you have a retainer relationship, it's very unlikely you will be your agency's (or even your account manager's) only client. The positive side of this is that it will enable the agency to bring new thinking from its experience across other brands and categories. But it will also mean they are working to multiple briefs and deadlines simultaneously, so be respectful when briefing them (however small a brief you think it is) and avoid quick turnarounds or (even worse) giving false deadlines. It's not uncommon for agency employees to regularly work very long hours. The industry is working hard to address this balance and to improve mental wellbeing, and we as clients can be part of this effort.

WHAT GOOD LOOKS LIKE

- Agencies are invited to all key future-focused meetings and are therefore fully aware of the vision, mission, corporate goals, strategic direction, brand positioning, objectives, goals and budgets of the organization

- No surprise when briefs arrive. Agency is already aligned and aware of brand's challenges and objectives, so more time can be spent on building disruptive creative ideas and proposals
- The agency is given an induction session so you can fully appreciate the role of each member of your agency team and go through their processes early on
- Briefs are of high quality and are complete, clear and inspirational; they are emailed, followed up face to face and then amended after the briefing to reflect any agency suggestions
- There is clarity on the agency's role and how they relate to other agency partners, so there are parameters for their scope and role, avoiding tension between agencies
- There is regular co-working in person or remotely to encourage the client and agency to become one team; there is understanding of the broad marketer's remit and the agency's skills are appreciated
- Quarterly and annually performance reviews are conducted – in both directions – to improve ways of working and performance, and keep the relationship fresh
- There is transparency – commercial numbers are shared, everyone works to hit the same financial targets, and there is clarity and a sense of teamwork
- There is commercial focus and alignment – proposals come with KPIs and initially calculated ROIs for both the short and long term, which makes for easier decision-making and sign-off

---

WHAT BAD LOOKS LIKE

- Agencies come in right at the end of the thinking process and are given limited context and poor briefs
- The most junior client-side team member writes and provides the briefs, so the long-term strategic context and SMART objectives are often missing and the agency's response is unlikely to be suitable, wasting everyone's time and investment

- Consolidated feedback is not given, and multiple iterations are made to the work, causing tensions and frustrations in the relationship and additional cost
- Agencies are remunerated on a restricted project rate but are expected to act as part of the team, be constantly available and respond to short lead times
- Agencies are treated as the lesser party (a supplier) or there is favouritism with some agencies being treated better than others
- Ways of working are not clearly defined, deadlines are not met, there are different working patterns and communications don't suit both parties
- Newly appointed agencies and new employees of the client aren't properly inducted and therefore lack context, brand knowledge and/or an understanding of the agency's process

QUESTIONS TO ASK YOURSELF

- What agencies do you currently enlist and why?
- Are they clear on your organization's background and its long-term strategic direction and goals?
- Are they clear on the role they play in relation to other agencies and your team in delivering the commercial goals?
- What are your ways of working? Could they be improved?
- What is your briefing process? How could you make it more inspirational and motivational?
- Is the agency servicing you or in partnership with you?
- Are they part of key meetings? Strategic planning? Defining brand positioning?
- Do they have access to all commercial data so they can calculate ROI and track performance?
- Are they remunerated at an appropriate level for the responsiveness you require?
- Do you hold regular performance reviews that assess both parties?

CAPTURE TIME: KEY DISCOVERIES

1.

2.

3.

WHAT THREE THINGS ARE YOU GOING TO DO TO IMPROVE?

1.

2.

3.

CHAPTER SUMMARY

I hope that this chapter has given you food for thought on how you or your team currently works with, manages and partners your agencies. I have aimed to provide you with the inspiration, motivation and tools to build strategic agency partnerships and relationships and to effectively brief and manage day-to-day relationships. In the next chapter we will look at ensuring the activities that agencies deliver are not only effective but also deliver against KPIs. We will also look at ROI and commercial acumen as a whole.

CHAPTER 6

LEADING THE COMMERCIAL AGENDA AND MEASURING EFFECTIVENESS

By now, I hope you will have noticed the number of times I have referred to the importance of marketers owning the commercial agenda. Commercial acumen is an essential competency that marketers need to possess, to ensure we can shift from being a support function to leading the commercial agenda.

In this chapter we will examine the key components of this competency: setting targets and forecasting, managing the profit-and-loss account (P&L), understanding key financial reports, and measuring marketing effectiveness through setting KPIs to ensure marketing investment is justified. We will also look at how to calculate ROI.

Having taught marketing metrics for many years and having trained teams to set KPIs, manage and monitor their effectiveness, and calculate ROI, I have found that business orientations vary, as does the commercial accountability of the marketing department. Therefore, whether you are already leading the commercial agenda or currently focused on communications, my aim is that this chapter will allow you to refocus and refresh your perspective, so you are empowered with the key knowledge to lead the commercial agenda, now or in the future.

If you want to be part of an organization, you have to speak the language of the organization … Marketers are excellent at customer insights but don't know about company insights – what the company does and how it makes things. These marketers have real career issues … Do two weeks of sales, go three weeks in a factory, go four weeks in distribution – whatever – so you understand what's going on. The language that's being spoken there is hugely important for you.

(Thomas Barta, Founder, The Marketing Leadership Masterclass)[37]

WHAT IS COMMERCIAL ACUMEN?

Commercial acumen means being financially literate, being able to read and interpret financial statements, and being able to advise and recommend changes that will positively change the financial shape and profit of the business. It entails understanding how your organization makes and spends money to make a profit and what levers to pull in your P&L.

As the orientation of business is moving from being production, sales and product led to being marketing led, marketers need to be able to truly lead the commercial side of the business and have the accountability and responsibility to deliver profit. We need to not only be aware of and understand the financial performance of the business but also understand how to influence its shape and convert its vision, strategy and tactical plans into profit.

This is broader than just managing your marketing investment. Of course, managing investment is important and a good place to start. However, what I mean is that you should have full accountability and control of managing the P&L. This involves understanding the importance marketing and the wider organization play within the P&L.

SETTING PROFIT TARGET AND FORECASTS

In the previous chapters we have looked at developing a long-term strategy, defining strategic choices and bringing these concepts to life. The first task is to determine when you will actualize your plans, how they will be phased and what they will be worth. A key component of this is forecasting units and/or demand against a set time frame or calendar of activities (whether for products or services). This tells you what will be sold when. Forecasting allows you to:

- Estimate revenues and profit
- Manage production demand (e.g. units and capacity) and therefore calculate the costs, staffing, resources and programmes that will be required

Inaccuracies can have an impact on:

- Resource allocation
- Budget
- Cash flow
- Production

There are two ways to develop a forecast:

- **Bottom up**: base rate, category or anticipated market growth rate, plus planned activity and seasonal peaks
- **Top down**: dictated volume, phased and broken down into key segments

Having created your forecast, you can then financially model the result to determine what this will generate for the business commercially. This will enable you to check you will hit any commercial targets and will also allow you to set monthly targets, providing clarity on delivery for you and your team. If your modelling reveals any likely short-fall, you can then adjust your plans ahead of roll-out.

Finally, models help you to create ROI calculations (as explained later in this chapter), and these can be used to support requests for capital expenditure or investment, either internally or externally.

UNDERSTANDING AND MANAGING THE PROFIT-AND-LOSS ACCOUNT

First of all, let's ensure we are clear what a P&L is. A P&L is a financial statement that allows you to see and understand the financial health of your business, business unit, brand or any area of the business for which you are accountable. It provides an overview of the revenue that is generated, any expenses that are incurred, and the profit or loss generated for any specific period of time. A P&L shows a company's ability to generate sales or turnover, manage its costs and deliver profit.

It is worth noting that terminology and descriptions of the various lines in a P&L may vary from organization to organization. Key elements may include:

- **Revenue/turnover**: sales value of a unit multiplied by the quantity of unit sold
- **Cost of goods/sales**: costs involved to produce the unit
- **Gross profit**: sales minus the cost of the goods sold (note that gross profit is also called profit before interest and taxation, or PBIT)
- **Operating costs**: costs required to run support functions such as admin, finance, customer services, sales and logistics
- **Operating profit**: gross profit minus total operating expenses
- **Net profit**: operating profit minus tax minus interest (note that net profit is also called net income)
- **Profitability**: this can be assessed from the P&L statement of the accounts, at a variety of levels: gross profit, net profit, earnings before interest, taxes, depreciation and amortization (EBITDA)

Specific lines may also be called out, such as:
- Marketing and advertising
- Customer payments or rebates
- Interest and loan payments or gains
- Taxes

I always said to people coming into the team: my objective is that in three or five years' time, if you want to leave the business, you should be able to walk into any venture capital with a business plan and raise finance. I openly shared the P&L with the team every single month. They all knew the targets [which I think helped because] even the term 'P&L' can bring people out in a cold sweat.

It's literally just about making more money and trying to control your costs or using your costs appropriately. It's just about knowing when to pull which lever, knowing when to go on a slightly deeper-cut promotion or spend more money above the line. Understanding how it all interacts [helps you to see that] no one should beat themselves up if they don't understand this. Start by doing it. If you can get access to the monthly management accounts, have a look at them.

(Emma Heal, Managing Director and Partner, Lucky Saint)[38]

INFLUENCING KEY ELEMENTS IN A PROFIT-AND-LOSS ACCOUNT

As a marketer, you need to not only be able to understand what you are seeing but also understand how you can adjust your P&L levers or lines to affect the profit number. *Table 6.1* gives you some examples of ways to do this, and the following sections explore these topics in more detail.

P&L LINE	HOW TO INFLUENCE IT
REVENUE, TURNOVER AND SALES	Increase the number of units sold (get existing users to buy more or get more users to buy)
	Increase sales in your existing market or target a different market (geographically or by category)
	Increase the price paid per unit (either existing or new users could pay more)
	Existing product development, new product development or enhanced experience
COST OF GOODS OR SERVICES	Reduce raw material costs or the cost to provide a service (procurement or suppliers)
	Find staff productivity efficiencies in production and delivering
	Find manufacturing efficiencies (e.g. run rates, time spent on processes)
OPERATING PROFIT	Reduce overheads, salaries and logistics (delivery and inventory management)
EARNINGS BEFORE INTEREST, TAXES, DEPRECIATION AND AMORTIZATION (EBITDA)	Investigate whether you can improve interest rates for loans and tax rates (although these are difficult to control)

TABLE 6.1 CHANGING THE SHAPE OF YOUR P&L

Turnover, revenue and sales

Let's start at the top and think about turnover. Your role as a marketer is to constantly grow your brand and increase the volume of what is being sold. As a marketer, you achieve growth through entering new markets, getting new users and getting your consumers to use you more frequently.

Think about an activity you currently do and how this will allow you to increase your volume, as well as how to maintain your existing users and volume – you don't want a leaky bucket (see *Chapter 2*).

A related concept is turnover. Getting your customers to pay more will in turn mean you will be able to charge more when you sell that product. In this way, you will naturally grow.

$$Turnover = Volume \times Unit\ Price$$

Cost of goods or services

The next line you can influence on the P&L is the cost of goods or services – in other words, the cost per unit. Whether you sell a product or a service, how much is it costing you as an organization to develop that product or service? Consider the following questions:

- How efficiently are you manufacturing your product?
- Are you looking at run rates, shift patterns and automation where applicable?
- What is the cost of raw materials coming into the business?
- What are the salaries?
- Is time being used efficiently and is it billable?
- What are the overheads or portioned overheads (the percentage of overheads that is attributed to your brand/division if you are part of a multi-branded business or holding) for your brand?

Check all of this is being effectively managed, because ultimately it will all affect the cost of your goods or, if you supply a service, what it costs to deliver that service.

Operating costs

If you are a one-brand business, all operating costs will be in your P&L. However, if you are a multi-brand business or part of a wider organization or holding group, a percentage of the operating costs may be attributed to you. The control you have over what is attributed to this line of the P&L will vary based on the size and scale of the business and your influence within it. Regardless, understanding what goes into your operating costs is useful to build your own awareness and understanding should costs need to be cut or efficiencies be needed in the value chain to increase profitability.

EBITDA

Tax levels set by the government in which you operate will be out of your control. However, it is useful to understand the impact any changes would have on your profit, as you may have to compensate for the effects elsewhere in the P&L. Interest gained from investments can help to generate profit.

PERIODIC REVIEWS AND BUILDING REMEDIAL ACTION PLANS

As your plan and forecast are rolled out, you will need to ensure that you are taking responsibility for delivering the required profit and any other commercial goals, and managing the P&L.

This means managing your P&L through periodic reviews – whether monthly, quarterly or annually – to ensure you are delivering on your budget, profit contribution and profit margin. If you are not, you can take charge to build remedial action plans, aligned with cross-functional teams, to close the commercial gap.

Most commonly held monthly, performance reviews provide a focus to ensure you are fully aware of your current position and performance. They enable you to see what is driving or causing the current situation (what?), what the implications will be (so what?), and what actions you can put in place to close existing or predicted commercial gaps (now what?). The following provides more detail on what is covered at each stage.

WHAT?

- Understand your performance for the month: what has driven growth (e.g. activity or launch) or stymied it (e.g. competitors' performance, customer relationships or delays)?
- Understand your performance versus your target or budget for the month, and whether you are on track to hit your annual goal

SO WHAT?

- Examine the implications of your performance for the month to date, for the year to date and in terms of hitting your year-end numbers

NOW WHAT?

- Investigate whether there are any remedial plans that you can put in place to close the gap in the budget and prevent further decline (e.g. change in investment or priorities)
- Communicate the performance to the wider business
- Ensure everyone is aligned with any remedial action plan and is clear on the implications this will have for cross-functional teams (production, sales, customer service, agencies, etc.)

It's important not to be hasty following a review. One month of bad performance does not mean that the strategy you have written needs to be screwed up and thrown in the bin. Your goal and vision may very well still hold true – you just may need to pivot or make changes to your existing plan to deliver them. You might need a different route of travel, but the destination will remain the same.

Too often, I have seen panic set in when a plan is not delivering performance. The sales team takes over, the marketing function's plans go out of the window, and short-term sales activity overrides any planned activity. Of course, we need both long-term and short-term thinking and activity to grow, but do try to balance the long-term effect (perception, price point erosion and full supply chain) of any quick, short-term burst to close the gap. Hold your own and remain in control – you've got this.

> [The] number one [thing to keep an eye on] is weekly performance. I call these BPN, or business performance management, meetings. I am directly involved in these or get the notes that come out of them, but either way I am all over the numbers on a week-to-week basis. I know friends who are in huge global FMCG [fast-moving consumer goods] companies in big global roles with major accountability for brands, and they're all over their numbers on a week-to-week basis. They understand where the market's moving, and it's just essential to do this.
>
> **(Emma Heal, Managing Director and Partner, Lucky Saint)**[39]

KEY FINANCIAL REPORTS

Businesses as a whole use certain key financial documents to report externally on their position and health. *Table 6.2* shows a list of these and provides definitions. You may find this useful if you need to understand board-level measures, shareholder reports or the health of your organization.

TERM	DEFINITION
CASH FLOW STATEMENT	Illustrates how an organization received and spent its money during a certain period. Sometimes called a 'consolidated funds statement.' You should have sufficient cash flow in the business to pay for goods, suppliers and staff ahead of receiving your revenue.
ASSETS	**Current/Short-Term**: something in the business that can be turned quickly into cash, i.e. stock, savings, etc.
	Fixed/Long-Term: also known as long term investments that would take time to convert into cash, i.e. machinery, land, etc.
	These can also be broken down further into:
	Tangible assets that you can physically touch, i.e. desks, equipment, etc.
	Intangible assets that can't be physically touched but still hold value, i.e. patents, trademarks, etc.
LIABILITIES	Monies owned that have already been committed, i.e. to insurance, bank loans, owed to vendors, etc.
BALANCE SHEET	A statement of how much the organization was worth at a specified point in time. It is made up of:
	Total assets: long term (property or long-term investment) + short term (money owed, in bank)
	plus
	Total liabilities – current: due in less than 12 months
	plus
	Total liabilities – long term: due in more than 12 months
	Combined, these represent the organization's total net worth.
CHAIR'S LETTER	A statement from a senior member of staff (such as the chair) giving their view on the organization's performance and the future.
AUDITOR'S REPORT	The accounts of organizations valued at, or earning over, a certain amount need to be independently audited. This report is the 'certificate' from the auditor.

TABLE 6.2 KEY FINANCIAL REPORTS

DEMONSTRATING THE EFFECTIVENESS OF SPENDING: KPIS AND METRICS

If you can't measure it, should you be spending it? I suggest that you spend 80% of your marketing investment on proven metrics and 20% on testing and learning. Of course, you can determine your split based on your budget and market conditions, consumer or customer task, and the level of testing and learning you are willing and need to do to disrupt in the market. Your allocations may also vary according to whether an area is working (customer-facing) or non-working (focused on production, fees and so on). However, the key thing here is knowing what to invest in and what you know will commercially deliver, either while live, in the short-term (post three months) and long term (post 12 months).

- **Strategic – long term**: related to the overall performance of an organization (e.g. shareholder value, ROI, branding and reputation)
- **Tactical – short term**: covering the next three or more months, these are measures to assess and improve areas such as customer satisfaction, loyalty rates and promotional effects
- **Campaign**: related to individual marketing activities undertaken by the organization, such as pay-per-click or direct mail campaigns

You will also need metrics with a more specific focus on your campaigns and activation, such as:
- **Campaign success**: to ensure objectives were met, understand what was achieved and what changed as a result of the campaign, and assess movement against SMART campaign objectives (see *Chapter 3*)

- **Campaign execution**: to assess how well the campaign was executed – for example, percentage of outlets which participated, number of samples distributed or number of actions executed within required timescales
- **Campaign efficiency**: cost per contact or lead generated within budget

WHAT ARE KEY PERFORMANCE INDICATORS (KPIS)?

KPIs are measurable values that define and demonstrate how effective certain key business initiatives or investments have been. They can be used across multiple levels – board (financial), strategic, tactical and campaign/activation. This ensures that each level is feeding into the next.

KPIs are important for several reasons:

- To ensure communication objectives have been met and assess whether the organization's strategy is effective
- To ensure campaigns have been executed efficiently
- To provide information for future marketing management decisions
- To prove to the organization that communication is effective and to protect communication budgets
- To capture learnings that will feed into future campaigns as part of the continuous improvement process (CIP) cycle

As long as you are learning you are not failing.

(widely attributed to Bob Ross)

Taking the time to set KPIs – which involves establishing a base rate or pre-measure ahead of activity going live – is key to determining what success looks like at the strategic, tactical and campaign levels. These then need to be communicated across the team, and research and data partners should be briefed to ensure that the required data collection initiatives are in place.

SHARE TIME

It is no good setting KPIs after activation has begun or without briefing research and insight partners before going live on what information you will need from them. This will mean that when the campaign is complete, they will only have access to continuous data sources to try to review the campaign's success.

SETTING AND MANAGING KPIS AND METRICS

Before your activity goes live, ensure that you complete the following steps:

- 12 weeks before the activity goes live, talk to your brand planner, research agency or data contacts, who will recommend exact measures to use
- Through a comparison with past activities, estimate the amount of movement your activity will cause
- Know your desired start and end points (your brand planner, research agency or data contacts will be able to guide you)
- Ensure the numbers are aligned with other agencies and internal teams
- Make sure your KPIs are trackable!

You will also need to ensure that each KPI has a planned method for data collection and analysis. This means doing the following:

- Nominate a data source
- Instruct the appropriate team(s) on what needs to be collected
- Allocate a budget for data collection
- Obtain the results
- Analyse the results
- Report findings and learnings

The reporting should ideally enable you to see:
- How well the investment in the campaign or activity has been spent and managed
- The sales uplift during the campaign or activity
- The short-term benefits and how these interlink with the delivery of the annual targets
- The long-term benefits and how these interlink with the long-term strategy and vision
- The learnings from the campaign or activity – would you do them again, do them differently or not repeat them, and why?

Finally, you will need to cascade these learnings:
- **Internally**: share the learnings with your team and other business functions, and ensure they will be available to future teams. Use the same methods as you would for sharing any other insight, such as the 6 Ss for storing insight (see *Chapter 7*).
- **Externally**: create case studies, report your findings to professional bodies and seek award nominations as appropriate. Help to raise the profile not only of what you or your brand have achieved but also of the industry or profession. Share the learning as widely as you can (ensuring that you protect intellectual property and sensitive information, of course).

SHARE TIME

I always say, spend money as if it were your own. Think of your brand or business as a house and your investment as home improvements. If you don't know whether an improvement would add value to your house in the short or long term, should you be spending the money? Of course, sometimes we need to do home improvements or invest to keep the house's foundations stable and to ensure it is safe before commencing other work. However, if you didn't know what impact an improvement would have, would you spend your own money on it?

Table 6.3 provides a list of suggested KPIs you can use to measure how effective a campaign has been. They are organized by activation or measurement type. These are just what's in my head – there will be more and some that are specific to your organization. Feel free to add them to the list – I have left a space for you to do so.

ACTIVITY	KPIs
ABOVE THE LINE (ATL)	Opportunities to see (OTS) and opportunities to hear (OTH)
	Reach
	Frequency
	Gross rating points
BELOW THE LINE (BTL)	Footfall
	Sales per outlet
	Samples distributed
	Coupons/prizes redeemed
	Point-of-sale (POS) sites and point-of-purchase (POP) coverage
BRAND	Financial
	Equity
	Associations
	Awareness
	Sentiment
	Perception
	Valuation
COMMERCIAL	Turnover
	Profit
	Margin
	Sales units
	Return on investment (ROI)
	Return on capital employed (ROCE)
	Growth versus the market
CONSUMER	Penetration
	Frequency
	Average weight of purchase (AWP)
	Category users – new and existing
	Perception
	Usage

CUSTOMER	Perception
	Net promotor score (NPS)
DIGITAL	Traffic
	Conversion
	Click through rate (CTR)
	Bounce
	Duration
	Likes
	Mentions
	Shares
	Comments and sentiments
	Reviews
EXTERNAL	Market share – valuation or volume
	Brand equity - Interbrand, brand Z
	Perception
INTERNAL	Volume or sales out
	Profit and margin
	Staff and NPS
	Employees' performance and attitude
PRODUCT AND INNOVATION	Percentage new products launched
	Profit margin
	Percentage revenue for new products launched from the total product mix
	Time to market
	Customer feedback

TABLE 6.3 KEY PERFORMANCE INDICATORS

CALCULATING ROI AND UNDERSTANDING LONG- AND SHORT-TERM GAIN

One of my passions is calculating ROI (sorry not sorry for my marketing geekiness level!). Doing so elevates marketing spend from a cost (which is so easily cut when sales performance isn't where it was forecast to be) to an investment. It allows the wider business to compare one investment with another.

A major bugbear of mine is when ROI terminology is used to describe effectiveness. In reality, they are oh so different:

- **Effectiveness**: this relates to the marketing investment that has been spent. How well did you spend that money? What did you get for your investment?
- **Return on investment**: this relates to the incremental value that spending generates for the business. It is always stated as a currency figure. For example, you might get back £1.30 for every £1.00 spent.

You have to be really proactive and think about how your money is going into ROI and get comfortable with understanding how it works. It's about knowing your customers, knowing your brand and knowing your numbers.

You need to demonstrate exactly how the activity you're going to do will drive a return, because if the CEO doesn't spend the money in marketing, they might spend it somewhere else ... How is this going to drive the bottom line? And there's obviously no point spending £50,000 on a marketing campaign or even £2,000 if you're going to eat into your profits – you're not going to make any money.

(Emma Heal, Managing Director and Partner, Lucky Saint)[40]

HOW TO CALCULATE ROI

To calculate ROI, you need:

- SMART objectives to define movement required within the set time frame
- Estimated net income generated by your campaign for this movement in this time frame
- The cost of investment

The formula is as follows:

Net Income from Investment =
Estimated Income – Cost of Investment
ROI = Net Income from Investment ÷ Cost of Investment

For example, if your estimated income were £250,000 and the cost of the investment were £50, you would calculate ROI as follows:

Net Income from Investment	= £250,000 – £50,000
	= £200,000
ROI	= £200,000 ÷ £50,000
	= £4

This means that for every £1 you spend, you get a return of £4. This is of course an extremely high ROI. You might do the same calculation and get a negative ROI – say, £0.50 for every £1.

What I always say is *do not* manipulate the numbers to get a positive ROI. Of course, reduce the cost or choose more effective mechanics (to increase your net income) if you are able. And, if you still want to go ahead with the activity despite the negative ROI, provide the broader context, such as a longer-term gain or to protect a relationship with a major customer.

I would suggest initially calculating ROI ahead of the investment being made, ideally as part of a marketing investment sign-off process, and then again three months after and a final time a year on. You can then capture and share the learnings as recommended above.

WHAT GOOD LOOKS LIKE

- There are cross-functional monthly performance reviews, with adequate data that allows you to understand the 'why' behind the performance and develop remedial action plans that keep you on track to hit your year's numbers
- The wider team and organization are aligned behind the reviews and data
- KPIs have been set that allow you to deliver your strategic, tactical and campaign objectives
- ROI is calculated both before and after an investment is made

WHAT BAD LOOKS LIKE

- A marketing calendar has been mapped without understanding how it relates to the business commercially, and there is no link with forecasts
- Marketing is not aware of or accountable for any elements of the financial targets or business performance
- There are no periodic reviews
- Marketing plans are aborted and replaced with sales promotions without consideration of the long-term impact and without cross-functional alignment
- Marketing activities are implemented without clarity on the anticipated ROI or KPIs
- Spending is consistent and always on, but there is no understanding of which element of investment is delivering the performance

- No reviews are held after activities to understand their benefits and gain learnings to feed into a CIP process

---

QUESTIONS TO ASK YOURSELF

- Do you know the lead measure that you are accountable for delivering?
- Is this lead measure based on turnover, cash number, profit number or margin, trading contribution, net revenue or number of units?
- Do you know how to translate your strategy and annual plans into a forecast and commercial budget (or P&L)?
- What financial position is the business in? Are you aware of its financial statements?
- Do you have access to your annual, quarterly and monthly P&L statements?
- Do you understand all of the lines on the P&L?
- Do you know how to leverage and influence each line on the P&L? Do you know which lines are most significant for your organization or brand?
- Do you know the difference between KPIs and ROI?
- Do you set KPIs before activation and measure progress before, during and after the campaign?
- Do you set aside funds for measurement initiatives?
- Do you spend 80% of your budget on proven metrics and 20% on testing and learning?
- Do you conduct a formal review of effectiveness and performance for each activity?
- Do you know how to calculate ROI? Do you do this ahead of activation (with a forecast) and then again after three months and after a year to enable you to understand the short- and long-term benefits?
- Is there an investment approval process in your organization?

- Do you need to establish one to ensure investment is being effectively spent and measured?

CAPTURE TIME: KEY DISCOVERIES

1.

2.

3.

WHAT THREE THINGS ARE YOU GOING TO DO TO IMPROVE?

1.

2.

3.

CHAPTER SUMMARY

In this chapter, we looked at the vital skill of being able to lead the commercial agenda. This means taking the reins of the organization and measuring effectiveness and return on marketing investment to demonstrate the value of our profession. In the next chapter, we will look at data and insight as a whole as this theme runs through everything we do as marketers.

CHAPTER 7

HOW TO DEVELOP AND LEVERAGE INSIGHT

In this chapter we will look at the true meaning of insight, examine why insight is important and how it forms the basis of all we do as marketers, and explore how to gain competitive advantage through insight. The chapter also gives an overview of the latest data sources (not themselves forms of insight but key sources of it) and allows you time to think about and audit your organization's existing data sources. We will also think about what you need to do to increase your organization's level of customer understanding. Finally, we will look at how to make insight actionable and ensure it is cascading throughout the whole organization.

THE TRUE MEANING OF INSIGHT

Insight is not data. Data shows you *what* happened. It's not until you mine it, usually putting it together with a variety of additional data sources, that you can find out *why* something happened. Usually insight holds a human truth – a psychological driver behind why something happened.

Insight can therefore be thought of as the capacity to gain an accurate and deep understanding of someone or something.

Insight comes from the act of mining and extracting information efficiently from a variety of data sources, which can be qualitative and/or quantitative. The process involves moving from something that is ubiquitous (data and observations) to something of value (insight).

> [Insight reveals] a person's true want, need or desire that a business can leverage.
>
> **(Richard Bambrick, Global Senior Insight Lead, Pentland Brands)**[41]

This quote from Richard Bambrick is revealing and it is worth exploring its components in detail:

- **Person**: customer or shopper
- **True**: the person would nod their head in acknowledgement as the want, need or desire would resonate with them – it would not be marketing jargon
- **Want, need or desire**: relating to human emotions or functional need
- **Business can leverage**: actionable in some way and has a benefit to the business (commercial or other type of benefit)

Julian Watson, an insight consultant at Labyrinth, says that insight has three parts:

- **Analysis**: you need to analyse data to get to the insight
- **Articulation**: a simple sentence that everyone gets on board with really quickly and, when you use it within your organization, it is understood straight away
- **Communication**: sharing the learnings in an engaging way with the wider organization[42]

Customer insight helps you to understand how your customers behave, but more importantly *why* they behave that way. It reveals their driving motivations. These can be collected from primary research (e.g. focus groups, panels, continuous data and ad hoc research) and secondary resources (e.g. market reports and trend studies), which can be gathered from inside or outside your organization. (Sources of data will be explored later on in the chapter.)

WHY IS INSIGHT IMPORTANT?

Insight is not only important – it is essential. The reason I have given it a whole chapter is because it sits across everything we do as marketers. The following sections explore some aspects of its broad application.

IT IMPROVES BUSINESS DECISION-MAKING

Insight allows decision-making to be based on facts and not assumptions. It allows you to validate the hypotheses and opinions of your sales team, internal staff members or customers. You can move from what I call a 'straw poll of one' to evidence supported by a robust sample from your current or target audience. Too much weight is often given to hearsay from an influential employee versus actual fact. Insight helps you to ensure that you are making the right choices based on fact-based discussion and not casual observations or assumptions.

For example, your market share might be going up or down, or you might be seeing a customer decline in a certain segment. Moving to an evidence-based conversation founded on data mining or data collection will enable you to understand what is happening better. Once you have mined the data, you can generate insight and thereby understand the true 'why' behind what is happening.

IT PROVIDES ACCESS TO THE VOICE OF THE CUSTOMER

If we don't listen to or seek out the voices of our customers, we are not marketing. We are unable to be customer oriented and we cannot fulfil the core definition of marketing – to anticipate or identify the wants and needs of our customers. Listening to the customer's voice is the foundation of every great service or product proposition, communication platform and activation plan.

IT IS CRUCIAL IN BUILDING AND EXECUTING STRATEGIC PLANS, AND MEASURING EFFECTIVENESS

The key ways to embed insight lie in the strategic planning process and the propositions that we bring to market. Insight also allows us to take a long-term view. These ways to embed insight play out in various situations.

Situation analysis

Insight is crucial when conducting a situation analysis (see *Chapter 2*). It helps us to understand both the macro environment and the micro environment. At the macro level, it helps us to predict and define external factors and trends that are outside our control now and in the long term (next three to five years), allowing us to identify opportunities we can leverage and threats we need to prepare for or defend against. At the micro level, it allows us to gain a deeper understanding of our competitors, suppliers, customers and so on, so that we are not only able to identify what has happened in our current position but also understand on a deeper level what might happen next and plan how we will respond.

Objectives, vision and mission

Insight helps us to develop objectives, a vision and a mission that we can own and that set us apart from the competition. It also helps us to set commercial and corporate objectives that are SMART (see *Chapter 3*), that are based on market conditions and that are stretching yet realistic.

Strategy and segmentation

In terms of segmentation, insight may allow us to understand the key factors in any market and thereby define which segments we should target and are best placed to go after. For example, if you are targeting other businesses, you will need to understand them based on their sector, size, quantity of employees, turnover and profit. Insight can also help you to understand who the key decision maker is and how well placed you are to serve them. For example, what is their age? Their role? Their demographic? You need to understand not just what they do but why they do it. Will they make decisions based on price alone or will they react on a deeper level, taking into account both their internal business's values and culture and their own views?

Let's take a moment to think about these ideas more broadly. If we are focusing our energies on the customer, who is the customer? Is it the end user? If not, who is the purchaser (e.g. spouse, parent or business owner)? Is it the person who's actually procuring the item? Is it the person who will use it? Or is it the person who holds the purse strings who makes the final decision? Or is it all of them? We need to remember that all of them are key in the decision-making process.

For example, it could be the receptionist. If we can't get past the receptionist, we're not going to access anybody else. So it's important to gain sufficient insight to understand the pathway our customers use to make a decision.

Brand or proposition

Building a brand or proposition should always be done as part of your strategic process. Your brand must be suitable to leverage the market or customer opportunity that you've identified, and it needs to enable you to win in specific market segments or areas of opportunity.

Insight is a vital part of this process. Your brand needs to be outward facing – in other words, based on what customers are looking for. You also need to have clarity on how your proposition makes you different from your competition.

This comes both from understanding your competitors on a deeper level and from understanding how your customers perceive you, who they are, what they are looking for and what their needs are.

This ensures you are building a proposition that is based on a combination of what potential customers do, what they want and need, and what you offer. The heartland sits in between these three factors (see *Figure 7.1*).

FIGURE 7.1 THE HEARTLAND OF AN EFFECTIVE PROPOSITION

PRESENTING YOUR PROPOSITION

I am often asked how to present propositions and customer needs. A great tool is Strategyzer (www.strategyzer.com), which lets you capture in one place how your product or service will address a customer need, including the pain (what is currently frustrating your customers) and gain (the benefits they will gain) points the product or service will satisfy.[43]

Marketing mix

Insight helps you to select the right marketing mix. You need to bring the right product to market at the right price, in the right place, at the right time and with the right communications. All of this can be developed and validated with insight.

Concept testing

Concept testing is a form of insight that allows you to measure customers' propensity to purchase again based on feedback about a proposed product and its price point.

You can also test your advertising by seeking insights on customers' emotions and thoughts and how to tailor your communications accordingly. Turf analysis enables you to determine the right product range and variants.

Key performance indicators and effectiveness

Setting realistic KPIs and tracking effectiveness are covered in a lot more depth in *Chapter 6*. However, it is important to remember that without data collection and the resulting insight, it would be impossible to set realistic KPIs or review metrics to improve your effectiveness.

USING INSIGHT TO CREATE COMPETITIVE ADVANTAGE

Often businesses invest heavily in insight as a way to lead their category or get ahead of their competition. Knowledge is power, after all, but only if the following points are followed. Otherwise, it just sits on a hard drive.

INSIGHT MUST BE ACTIONABLE

Once you have mined the appropriate data and found your 'aha' moment, you need to move from insight (what you have discovered) and think about the 'so what' and 'now what' to move to actionable insight. This means determining what you can do and will do with the insight. This may be something that your competitors have not yet discovered or actioned.

INSIGHT MUST BE ACTIONED WITH PACE

Don't sit on it. I have seen too many organizations spend time, money and energy on developing insight to define new propositions, but then take years to phase them in. Or, due to infrastructure complexity, the process of getting to market takes too long, meaning more agile brands and challengers get there first.

YOU NEED BRAVERY AND CONVICTION

Bravery and conviction are needed to take action and either bring your proposition to market or make the change your insight has highlighted. Sometimes bravery is needed internally to share what you have found and fight to give it the airtime it needs. You might also need bravery to take action externally.

The reason Amazon overtook their competition was that they had the bravery to use the insight they had on their customers' buying behaviour and patterns. And, then, they had the conviction to physically move the customer's anticipated next purchase closer to their location ahead of them ordering it. This is how Amazon Prime was born.

The qualities of bravery and conviction are covered further in *Unit 2*.

YOU MUST HAVE DIFFERENT DATA SOURCES FROM YOUR COMPETITORS

The chances are that you probably have a lot of data sources that are the same as those your competitors are using – for example, industry reports, and continuous or quarterly performance data – and that are sourced from the same provider. You need to think about what you have that's unique to you that allows you to mine to a deeper level or provides a different perspective or more richness.

USING DATA SOURCES

In order to develop actionable insight, the first step is to collate and gather data. Pose the question or hypothesis you are looking to answer. You may be able to answer it with the data you already have. If not, do you know about all the sources available to you?

WHAT TYPES OF DATA ARE AVAILABLE?

Data or market research methods have both expanded the amount of data available to us and increased the speed with which we can collect it. An omnibus survey (a series of questions on a variety of subjects) that used to take two or more weeks can now be done in a matter of days or hours. Some methods even allow overnight or real-time feedback.

The following sections explore the major types of data and their sources.

Qualitative versus quantitative research

Insight can be gained through both qualitative (based on opinion) and quantitative (based on numbers or facts) data sources. For example, qualitative research might allow you to collect the opinions of a group of individuals via a focus group, whereas quantitative research yields insights such as "X% of our customers believe this to be an issue."

Qualitative research generally aims to determine attitudes and the reasons behind them. Examples of qualitative research methods include:

- Focus groups or group discussions
- In-depth interviews
- Workshops
- Customer panels
- Mystery shoppers
- Observations
- Accompanied visits or shopping trips

Quantitative research is more structured and generally provides information on the numbers of people who do something or feel a certain way, often from a robust sample size. Examples of quantitative research methods include:

- Exit interviews
- Field trials
- Omnibuses
- Surveys (online, by telephone or face to face)
- Observations that are recorded quantitively (e.g. the number of times something happens)
- Eye-tracking
- Psychometric testing
- Social media monitoring and mining

Primary versus secondary research

Another way of categorizing data is into primary and secondary sources. Primary research is research that you commission yourself to fit your own needs. Secondary research is existing research that has previously been gathered by others. It may be in the public domain and is likely to also be accessed by competitors and the wider industry. Although it is useful for identifying the market context, size and trends, it is unlikely to allow you to understand the 'why' or gain a competitive advantage.

Sources you can use for primary research include:

- Customer relationship management (CRM) systems – purchasing, behavioural and profiling data
- Sales figures
- Customer satisfaction results
- Customer complaints records
- Effectiveness data from activations (ecommerce, physical or digital traffic, etc.)
- Social media channels – using the wealth of data already known about an individual, including their friendship groups and product preferences
- Web and app analytics, and social media analytics

Sources of secondary research include:

- Press (national and local)
- Market reports (e.g. published by Mintel), business periodicals and academic journals
- Trade press
- LinkedIn
- Published competitors' information
- Economic reports
- Reports by professional bodies (e.g. the Chartered Institute of Marketing, the Institute of Promotional Marketing and the Advertising Standards Agency)
- Social media listening and monitoring

RESEARCH TOOLS AND METHODOLOGIES TO CONSIDER

- Heat maps
- Eye-tracking capabilities (e.g. via mobile)
- Behavioural measurement and behavioural science
- Biometrics (e.g. use of smart watches to track physiological responses to advertising in-store)
- Webcam-based interviews
- Mobile ethnography
- Live audience response systems and online panels
- Online collaboration tools (e.g. using video, instant messaging or apps)
- Online communities and expert and customer panels
- Real-time surveys
- Streetbees (see https://www.streetbees.com)

There are so many digital solutions out there that are labelled as providing artificial intelligence or using smart algorithms to pick up movements in facial expressions or uncover human behaviour, and they are great. But I think there has got to be a balance between some older methods and some of these new methods. The future of market research and insight for me is the middle ground that takes on board the learnings of speed and agility and the creativity, but still gives the rigour when necessary.

(Julian Watson, Insight Consultant, Labyrinth Marketing)[44]

CONDUCTING A DATA AUDIT

Conducting a data audit will allow you to see where you are using data well and where you might be able to close gaps in your knowledge by selecting better sources of data.

On the following pages, I have given you a few exercises to allow you to review what you collect or have already collected.

You don't always need to gather new data – you may find that you have forgotten about useful sources or have not used some to their full potential. For example, perhaps you commissioned some research but didn't mine or fully exploit it after the initial study.

SHARE TIME

I have seen a whole host of scenarios in which organizations invested heavily in continuous data (i.e. focused on tracking performance and what had already happened) but rarely spent time and money examining what might happen next or getting a deeper understanding of their customers' needs. I have also seen organizations use only secondary and internal data and wonder why they struggled to get ahead of their competition.

I was once asked to train a retailer's marketing function on strategic planning. Ahead of the training, I asked the management team what lead measure they were chasing, so I could ensure the team was building SMART objectives based around it. During the training, when I audited the data sources with the team, I discovered that they weren't tracking this lead measure at all. Instead, they were tracking a whole host of other continuous data sources, which they had been doing for many years. We need to ensure that the data we collect is aligned with the objectives we are striving to achieve.

Review your data sources

Let's start by reviewing what data sources you collect. Use *Table 7.1* to capture your current data sources.

Qualitative	Quantitative
Primary	Secondary

TABLE 7.1 YOUR DATA SOURCES

QUESTIONS TO ASK YOURSELF TO IDENTIFY GAPS

- Having listed your data sources in *Table 7.1*, are there any obvious gaps?
- Is there a mix of qualitative (what customers think and feel) and quantitative (based on facts and numbers) data that you can use to validate your hypotheses?
- Are you collecting all the primary data that is necessary and appropriate?
- Is there a balance between secondary (available to all) and primary (unique to you) data?
- Are there any data sources you no longer need or don't need to collect as frequently?
- Could this investment be better spent elsewhere to close some of the knowledge gaps?

Map the customer journey

The next step is to map your customer journey, either alone or as a team, with all the data sources you have available to you. For each target audience or customer persona, map their journey, from identifying the need to after the purchase.

1. Define the target audience or persona for which you are mapping the journey
2. List the key stages of their journey to purchase – examples for both consumers and businesses are as follows:
   › Consumers: recognize problem, search for information, evaluation, purchase, post-purchase
   › Businesses: recognize problem, develop product specification to solve, search for product and suppliers, evaluate products and suppliers, evaluate products and suppliers relative to the specification
3. List what you know happens at each stage or each touchpoint:
   › The information they are looking for at each stage
   › Where they go to get the information
   › Who they involve or bring with them
   › When and where this happens
4. Having mapped each journey, record what data source you have for each touchpoint
5. For each data source, record whether it is:
   › Fact (validated by a data source)
   › Observation (have seen but not robustly or quantitatively validated)
   › Assumption (assumed behaviour not based on fact or observation)
6. Now look at each journey and consider the following:
   › Where are there gaps in your data sources?
   › Where have assumptions been made that need to be validated?

> › How will you close these knowledge gaps? Which sources and methodologies will you use? What might it cost?
> › Which data sources do you believe give you a competitive advantage versus your competition (both direct and indirect competition)?

Select data sources and methodology

The ultimate goal is for the data we collect to use the methodology that gets us closest to the actual behaviour of our customer s – how they truly think, feel and behave. It doesn't need to be the most innovative source – just the one that gets us closest. The AFECT model provides five criteria for evaluating the psychological validity of market research:[45]

1. **Is this an analysis of behaviour?** Does the data indicate what people currently do now? Always begin with sales data and (covert) behavioural observation. Asking people what they have done can also be useful, but the longer the time since this happened, the worse recall and accuracy are likely to be.

2. **What frame of mind were the respondents in?** How close is the research process and methodology to the actual context the customer is in when deciding on a purchase? Using an artificial process, methodology and context will affect a respondent's frame of mind as the situation will be very different from that of the real world.

3. **Were environmental cues present?** When it comes to the value of an insight, understanding to what extent environmental cues were present at the time is crucial. If they weren't present, a very different response is likely to occur when they are.

4. **Was the research covert?** When people know they are being observed or measured, they behave differently.

5. **Was the response time frame realistic?** Many decisions to purchase consumer goods are made swiftly.
Elongating this for research purposes does not reflect
actual behaviour.

There is an incredible number of data sources out there
– but it is also incredible how little companies and their
leaders pay attention to them, let alone use them. They are
often collecting the same sources of data on a continuous
basis that show them how they are performing but not taking the time to review what new data sources they should
consider or why what is happening is happening. It's the
root cause that is insight and not the data source.

THE ETHICS OF COLLECTION AND STORAGE

On the topic of data collection, a final word is needed on
the importance of ensuring that the data you gather is collected for a legally sanctioned purpose. We live in a digital
age with access to big data, but you shouldn't collect data
just because you can. I often find that the more that is collected, the less likely it is to be analysed. It is best to focus
your energies on the data you actually need.

Additionally, you must always collect and store data ethically and in line with relevant local laws, such as the General Data Protection Regulation (GDPR). If in any doubt,
please check with a lawyer (I am not qualified to provide
legal advice or interpretation).

Let's now look at behavioural science, which offers various options for understanding customers' decision-making.

BEHAVIOURAL SCIENCE

In marketing, behavioural science focuses on truly understanding purchasing decisions and usage habits by understanding the underlying (often hidden) drivers of people's behaviour. This allows marketers to build propositions that meet customers' needs more completely.

Behavioural science isn't an entirely new concept, but its application to marketing and research is increasing in popularity. Its methodology allows you to understand customers' behaviours, habits and decision-making by using empirical data, evidence and facts rather than intuition, observation or assumptions (for example, when we analyse someone's behaviour, we tend to gather observations based on what we want to see).

SYSTEM 1 AND SYSTEM 2 THINKING

Behavioural science has been rising in popularity since the release of the book *Thinking, Fast and Slow* by Daniel Kahneman, Nobel Prize winner in Economics.[46] In this book, Kahneman distinguishes between two ways in which the brain processes information: System 1 (automatic, emotional and fast) and System 2 (effortful, cognitive and slow).

In System 1 thinking, our brain uses shortcuts to avoid having to process huge amounts of data. There are three types of shortcut:

- **Heuristics**: effectively rules of thumb that allow us to replace a complicated evaluation with a much shorter one, such as "If I see x, it's likely that y is also true"
- **Defaults**: for example, "I chose to buy that product last time and it wasn't bad so I'll just do the same thing again"
- **Biases**: systematic ways that our brain jumps to (often faulty) conclusions

These shortcuts happen so quickly that it is often only after we have reached a conclusion that we then work out our justification for it. Because of this speed, we're not aware of what is happening, although we think we have made a rational decision. Estimates of how often we use System 1 thinking in everyday life vary, but it could be as high as 95% of the time.[47]

In contrast, System 2 thinking is rational and considered. We invest time and effort in evaluating multiple options.

Kahneman's model is very helpful in enabling us to understand how people make decisions about brands. It updated our thinking from perceiving the human brain as an information-processing machine that makes decisions driven principally by facts and only weakly influenced by emotions, to one where emotions or shortcuts are often the primary drivers of behaviour. I'm sure this will resonate with most of us from our own decisions.

This reflects what we see in customers' interactions with brands, namely that they look to connect with aspirations, values and beliefs (i.e. emotions). Kahneman's behavioural science model recognizes that most decisions are made automatically, with little or no conscious thought (mental shortcuts).

We, as marketers, can move from focusing on commercial rationales (such as 'How much will a customer be prepared to pay for this?') to focusing more on the mechanics of decision-making – whether that is 'How much do customers or consumers like and connect with this?' or even how customers look to make decision-making as easy and effortless as possible. As marketers, we therefore need to understand the importance of emotional brand associations that are built up over time. Tactics like pricing are not the be all and end all.

In short, we need to consider how people really think, feel, behave and make decisions in the real world rather than how we'd like them to in our marketing utopia.

System 1 heavily uses somatic markers, the physical imprints that your body stores of the emotion it experienced during previous events. These are called more quickly to your brain than your brain can process new information. So you almost have an emotional response and then post-rationalize what has driven it.

(Kate Socker, Twigged Innovation)[48]

THE BENEFITS AND USES OF BEHAVIOURAL SCIENCE

Behavioural science has multiple benefits and practical applications. For example:

- **Accuracy**: understanding actual behaviour, based on empirical data and context-specific experiments, removes the potential for human error, interpretation and subjectivity
- **Insight**: consciously build the cognitive drivers behind behaviours into concepts and designs
- **Advertising or comms development**: build behavioural learnings into your approach – after all, the desired outcome of communications is usually a behavioural response

Ask your agencies what is in fact interpretation and what is evidence-based and relevant to your specific context. As behaviour is so contextually dependant, just because it's worked elsewhere doesn't mean it's the best route.

Find the right partners who can help you really apply the knowledge and who are connected with the behavioural scientists in academia. They're not only more likely to be committed to an evidence-based approach but will also have access to the latest developments.

(Kate Socker, Twigged Innovation)[49]

MINING DATA TO DEVELOP ACTIONABLE INSIGHT

The term 'data mining' refers to the process of analysing data to gain insights, and this is where the magic happens.

In data mining, the aim is to look at the data as objectively as possible, sceptically examining how accurate it is and looking at the differences as well as the similarities. My favourite method of mining data is also the simplest. The Five Whys is a technique in which you interrogate an inference or fact that has been identified or that is presented to you, to get to the root cause of why it happened. The idea is that five is the number of 'whys' it takes to move from observation to root cause.

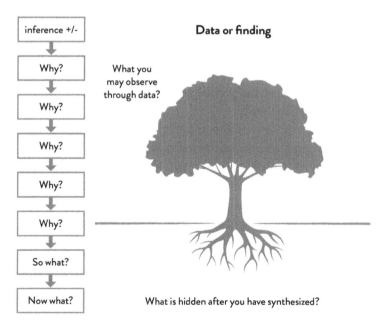

FIGURE 7.2 5 WHY'S MODEL

As an example, take a look at the following:
- **Inference**: identified value growth in cat food
- **Why?** Premium brands of cat food are in growth, driving the value
- **Why?** Cat owners are willing to pay a premium for cat food
- **Why?** Because cats are part of their family
- **Why?** Because they like to treat their cats and give them the best
- **Why?** Because they feel bad for leaving them at home all day
- **So what?** Cat owners want to treat their cats because they are part of the family and to alleviate guilt from leaving them at home alone
- **Now what?** Use this human truth in future communication and expand your premium range

I often get asked, "What if I get there before five whys, or what if it takes me six or seven whys?" If you need more than five, that's fine – ask as many whys as you need. However, I would say that if you get there in less than five, you may not have gone deep enough unless you started with a customer truth already.

The moment at which you feel that you have uncovered a fresh insight is commonly known as an 'aha' moment. The 'aha' moment usually triggers an emotional feeling or gut response that allows you to know when you've arrived at a new discovery (this is probably the only circumstance in which I will allow the gut to be a form of auditing tool). The 'aha' moment reveals something that hasn't been brought to the forefront of your attention before, and it shows you not *what* is happening but *why* it is happening. It's usually a psychological or emotional reason why someone acted in a certain way. This discovery, or any hypothesis made around the 'why,' may need to be validated further, depending on the data sources available or what was used as you moved through the amended Five Whys model.

So, once you have defined the insight, what next?

PRESENTING YOUR INSIGHT TO THE BUSINESS AND DEFINING HOW IT SHOULD BE USED

Once you have identified an insight (what), you will need to define how it can be leveraged by your organization (so what). This is what makes an insight actionable. What that means is that there will be a key element of your insight that your organization can identify as an opportunity or issue that it wants to leverage.

There will normally be a tension point between what you've uncovered and what you need to do within the organization (now what) to allow it to capitalize on the insight. This may require some additional work, buy-in, capital, alignment and so on. Don't shy away from the energy this takes, as bringing products and services to market based on insight is our moment to shine as marketers.

You may also need to refine and validate any hypothesis you have developed using the Five Whys, so that it is believable and robust. It is important that you're not working off assumption but off fact.

QUESTIONS TO ASK YOURSELF:
MAKING AN INSIGHT ACTIONABLE

- **What?** What insight have you identified?
- How will you present the insight to your organization?
- **So what?** What could this bring to the organization financially? In the short term and long term? For the brand? For your customers/retailers to aid sell-in and distribution gains?
- **Now what?** What do you propose the organization should do? What do you need to bring this to life? Capital? Resources? Time?

CROSS-FUNCTIONAL USE OF INSIGHT

Having defined the insight, it is essential to ensure that you make it shareable and accessible for everyone in your organization.

The whole organization needs to have a deep understanding of the customer, especially those members of the organization who are customer-facing. Being able to better understand who customers are and what they need, value, think, feel and do will help sales, customer services, product development and many other departments. You as a marketer hold the key to the voice of the customer, and you must ensure this is understood throughout the whole organization. Sharing insight to bring the customer to life is central to achieving this.

In order for the insight to be used and reflected in the whole company's thinking, it is important to share it in a way that the whole organization can access and interpret. Information must be motivating, easily understood and easily accessed by all. This means delivering your message in a way that considers all four learning styles (written, verbal, visual and kinaesthetic – i.e. learning by doing).

You need to embed the customer's voice within the organization, so it's not just data on a slide or a detail dropped into your strategy. Storytelling is a great way to do this and is covered in *Chapter 9.*

STORING INSIGHT

After you have shared your insight, you need to store it so that it is accessible and searchable for everyone in your organization. Too often, I see insight leaving the building when employees leave, especially ad hoc studies that are stored on individuals' hard drives. A marketing knowledge information system (MKIS) is a great way to ensure there is a central, searchable location with access for all. Sharing insights in an MKIS not only makes it easier for the next brand guardian or colleague to access it but also avoids duplicated studies or data being commissioned unnecessarily, wasting time, money and resources.

THE 6 Ss: INSIGHT AND KNOWLEDGE MANAGEMENT CHECKLIST

I have defined the 6 Ss, which outline the key steps required to embed actionable insights in your organization:

- **Synthesize** your findings to define and identify the key actionable insight
- **Share** your findings with your wider team so you can mine the data together and identify the insights
- **Story:** has the data or presentation of the insight been digested and the key themes and statistics pulled out to tell a story?
- **Scale** the insight with the wider organization so everyone can understand the voice of the customer and be motivated by it
- **Store** the insight in an MKIS so it is accessible for all now and in the future
- **Strategy:** ensure your insight is used as the basis of any strategic development plans

WHAT GOOD LOOKS LIKE

- Your data sources allow you to have a complete understanding of your market and the entire customer journey, enabling a full and deep-rooted emotional understanding of key touchpoints
- You use a mix of data sources, including some that give you a competitive advantage and some that reflect your lead measure
- Data is mined and built into actionable insights, and the next steps are outlined before being shared in a motivational and resonating way with the wider team
- There is clarity on what questions need to be answered
- You and your organization act with pace and bravery in bringing insight-fuelled propositions to market
- Data and insight are used to have fact-based conversations from day to day and throughout the strategic planning process

WHAT BAD LOOKS LIKE

- Continuous data sources are reviewed only at inference level, looking only at performance and not what has driven it
- Reams of statistics are forwarded to teams without insights being mined, key insights being highlighted or 'what next?' being answered
- Hypotheses are not validated and often used in absence of true insight
- Insights are not accessible and are not shared with the wider organization to enrich all colleagues' understanding of the customer
- Insights are lost to the organization when staff leave

QUESTIONS TO ASK YOURSELF

- Are you aware of and do you understand the data sources and methodologies available to you, and do you know what information these data sources will provide?

- Do you or your team have the necessary skill set for data mining or can you outsource this?
- Are you able to define the research questions that need to be answered? Can you identify existing or new data sources that will answer the questions?
- Are you able to analyse and interpret both qualitative and quantitative data?
- Are you able to make your insights ('aha' moments) actionable so your organization is clear on what it could and should do?
- Are you able to map fact-based customer journeys?
- Are you able to develop a deep, emotionally rooted understanding of your customer? Can you consolidate and communicate this to your organization?
- Are you able to translate your analysis into key findings and share these with the wider organization in a way that is accessible, digestible and understood?
- Are you acting with pace and bravery to bring the actions from the insight to life?
- Are you able to advise on what data your organization should and could be collecting? Are you able to develop a process for you and your team to brief others (where necessary), collate, mine, share and action?
- Are you using insight to help you and others be the voice of the customer?

QUESTIONS TO ASK FOR YOUR ORGANIZATION

- Are we collecting the right data sources to allow us to understand our customers, market and competitors?
- What is our insight process? How do we collect, receive, extract, mine data?
- How is our data presented, used, stored, accessed by others or in the wider organization?

- Do we have a balance between data that provides facts about what has already happened (performance and actual behaviour) and data that gives information on what is likely to happen next (stated and claimed behaviour)?
- Do we understand not only who our customers are but also what they value on a deep emotional level?
- Do we understand our customer's journey? Do we have data sources for each stage?
- What gaps do we have and how will we close them? Which data sources are needed?
- Which of our sources of data are the same as those of our competitors? Do we have anything that gives us a unique perspective?
- Where is our data stored? Is it accessible to all? Is it easy to find?
- Do we use insight at every stage of our strategic planning process?
- Do we have an MKIS?

CAPTURE TIME: KEY DISCOVERIES

1.

2.

3.

WHAT THREE THINGS ARE YOU GOING TO DO TO IMPROVE?

1.

2.

3.

CHAPTER SUMMARY

In this chapter, we covered the importance of developing and leveraging true insight across all we do as marketers. This enables us to understand the voice of the customer, their true behaviours and their decision-making process.

In this chapter, we looked at the difference between data and insight, reviewed data sources available, learnt how to mine data to deliver true actionable insight and the importance of developing and leveraging true insights across all we do as marketers. This enables us to understand the voice of the consumer and customer, their decision-making process and their true behaviours on a deep-rooted emotional level.

In *Unit 1* as a whole, we focused on the technical skills we need as marketers today. In *Unit 2*, we will look at not *what* we do but *how* we do it. The following chapters start by looking at how to understand your customer on a more deep-rooted, emotional level. They then examine the behaviours of a strong marketer, including the skills of aligning, motivating and leading all stakeholders internally and externally; the role of a marketing leader; and how to provide clarity when leading and motivating teams.

UNIT 2

Soft Skills and Leadership Skills

WHAT IS COVERED?

In *Unit 1* we looked at the technical skills marketers of today need to possess – *what* you need to do. In Unit 2, we will look at *how* you do it – the soft skills and behaviours that I believe marketers should possess and demonstrate, almost as second nature, in both understanding their customers on a deep-rooted, emotional level and bringing their plans to life. We will also look at the role of leadership and specifically the skills of marketing leaders, whether you are leading a campaign, brand, team or whole function.

Additionally, we will look at how to motivate your team or function by providing clarity on your vision for the team or function. We'll also look at how to deliver this by outlining both their role in delivering the overall goals for the business, and what they need to deliver individually, through capability frameworks, job descriptions and career development plans. Finally, we will look at how to embed all of this in the day to day.

In summary, we will cover:

- **Soft skills**: the personal attributes needed for success in your role
- **Leadership behaviours**: how you respond or act in a particular situation
- **Leadership skills**: how to lead a group of people or an organization

WHY IS THIS IMPORTANT?

It is not only what we do (our technical skills) but also how we do things that creates the route to success and enables us to drive change and get results for ourselves and our brand and organization. We are the voice of the customer and therefore need to be able to understand them on a deep-rooted, emotional level – better than our competition – to win their hearts and minds. To make any change happen, we need to be able to inspire those around us and have the resilience, conviction and can-do attitude to bring our plans to life.

Leadership is a skill that can no longer be a 'nice to have' or left for the few natural born leaders, as marketing is now the function that needs to lead. Whether we are leading the organization, the brand, a cross-functional team, a project, a campaign or something else, leadership is now part of our everyday working life and a skill we can develop over time.

Our expectations of work have also changed – it's no longer a job but a career. And, as marketers, we are now more stretched than we have ever been, due to our role breadth and increased accountability. Therefore, providing clarity, motivation and support to our teams and those in our care has never been more important.

You need to have leadership capability, understand how to communicate on a fundamentally different level, really understand what responsibility and accountability are, have the curiosity, the ambition and all the softer stuff. If you don't have that, it doesn't matter how good your technical skills are.

(Sherilyn Shackell, Founder and Global CEO, The Marketing Academy)[1]

CHAPTER 8

UNDERSTANDING YOUR CUSTOMER ON A DEEP-ROOTED, EMOTIONAL LEVEL

In this chapter we will look at the soft skills and behaviours that marketers need to understand our customers on a deep emotional and psychological level. These skills will also benefit our relationships with our colleagues. I love to see these skills in a marketer, as they mean the marketer is likely to be truly immersed and in sync with their customers and their profession, and reflect the role of today's marketer. They not only know and truly understand the customer but also speak up to ensure they are the voice of the customer, to ensure the organization is delivering against the customer's wants and needs.

What we won't cover in this chapter are the soft skills that are often listed in any marketing job advertisement, such as 'self-starting,' 'collaboration,' 'ambition' and 'strong communication.' These are of course still relevant and important. However, if I may be so bold, these are parity points – qualities you would hope to see in any marketer and in most functions' job descriptions. What this chapter focuses on are the key soft skills and behaviours that I look for specifically in passionate consumer- and customer-connected marketers – those that separate the best from the rest, if you like.

CURIOSITY

WHAT IS CURIOSITY?

Curiosity is the instinctive desire to know something. It is the driving force behind the wish to have a deeper understanding through exploring and questioning.

WHY IS IT IMPORTANT?

Research shows that lifelong curiosity helps us in both our working lives and our relationships. Curiosity is strongly linked to creativity, problem-solving abilities and relationship quality. It is also the catalyst for understanding human behaviour – not *what* is happening but *why* it is happening.

We are all born nosy – it's crucial in the early years of our development. However, as we learn more about those things that we were once curious about and they become part of our everyday lives, sometimes our natural curiosity starts to slip.

As marketers, we can't afford to lose this essential skill, as if we're not curious, we will never ask "Why?" Therefore, we will never get to a deep-rooted understanding and in turn emotional connection with our consumers and customers. We need to understand our customers beyond their job role, age, demographics and what they do at a surface level. To understand *why* they do what they do, we need to comprehend their thinking, feelings, beliefs and values, and what drives their decision-making.

We also need to use our curiosity internally to understand how our organization, our function and the people within them work and operate. This will improve our processes so we have a greater competitive advantage and more success at bringing our ideas to market.

> [A marketer should have] a huge, deep curiosity for the business they're in, how the business works, what makes it tick, how the business makes money and the role marketing plays in helping the success of that organization.
>
> I'm on the lookout for people that are very curious, keen to keep learning, keen to really roll up their sleeves, get within the organization, work with finance, work with the relevant strategy and sales teams – just get their arms around what makes a business successful and the role marketers can play, not just in how things operate today but how things could operate in a better, even more improved, enhanced environment moving forward.
>
> (Pete Markey, CMO, Boots UK)[2]

Be more curious and feel uncomfortable for a bit longer.

(Kate Socker, Founder, Twigged Innovation)[3]

SHARE TIME

The first thing I do in any training session is introduce myself. Trainers are taught to do this to establish credibility with the delegates in the room. The patter goes something like this: "Hi, I'm Abby Dixon and I'm your trainer today. I'm a Chartered Marketer and fellow, and I've been training for over a decade across the marketing discipline. I've led growth, advised organizations on how to grow, and trained marketers and their teams across many household brands and industries [cue slide with the brands' logos sprawled across it] and I also help agencies [cue slide showing the agencies and professional bodies I help]."

But then I look to the room and ask, "Who is trying to work me out? Put your hand up."

It's those marketers who don't put their hand up that I really worry about (although I also realize they may just be shy or fear failure). I worry because I strongly believe that one of the key skills of marketing is to identify customer needs. Therefore, you need to be curious about humans, their behaviours, and what they value and believe so you can truly connect with them on an emotional level. Marketing is the profession that satisfies the wants and needs of customers. Do you know what they truly want and need?

WHAT GOOD LOOKS LIKE

For consumers, you try to work them out by wondering:

- Who are they? Where do they live? Who do they live with?
- What are they doing? Why are they doing those things? What are their drivers, both rational (thinking) and emotional (feeling)?
- What do they value? What are their beliefs?
- What are they looking for?

- What's driving them? What they are doing in their day-to-day lives?
- What are their key pain and gain points?

For customers, you try to work them out by wondering:
- Who are they? Where do they live? Who do they live with?
- What is their professional background? What is their role?
- What is their motivation to get out of bed every morning?
- Who makes the decisions?
- What is key in their decision-making criteria, both rational and emotional?
- What do they believe is important in life? In a supplier?
- What are their company's values? Why did they choose to work there?

I could go on, but the key principle is to understand not just *what* they are doing but *why* they are doing it. This is where the insight lies.

QUESTIONS TO ASK YOURSELF TO IMPROVE YOUR CURIOSITY

- Do you people-watch, thinking about what they are doing and why?
- Do you people-watch in a variety of locations?
- Do you do this for your target consumer/customer?
- Are you willing and brave enough to question everything and to ask "Why?" until you understand more?
- Do you read, watch and explore a variety of topics, subjects and areas of interest? Or ones that are of interest to your target audience or customer?
- Do you do something different as often as you can? (It can be anything from taking a different route to work to eating lunch in a new spot to trying out a new artist or music type. Broadening your sources of stimulus will break you out of your routine and force you to be more aware and therefore more curious.)

EMPATHY

WHAT IS EMPATHY?

Another soft skill that is key to truly getting into the hearts and minds of your customers is to have empathy.

There are different levels to be considered, starting with sympathy, which is where you share the same feelings of another person.

Empathy is the ability to understand and share feelings with others by putting yourself in their shoes and understanding things from their perspective.

Finally, to be empathetic is to possess the ability not only to understand, but also to absorb and feel the same emotions that another person is feeling.

WHY IS IT IMPORTANT?

Empathy has two key benefits in the workplace for marketers.

Firstly, it enables you to better understand and relate to others. This benefits your working relationships – internally with individuals and your teams and colleagues, and externally with agency partners, suppliers and customers.

An associated benefit is that you will become known for being approachable and likeable, because others will benefit from your attentiveness, your understanding and the time you give. They are also likely to reward your time and support with improved levels of commitment, loyalty and motivation, and more deliverables.

Secondly, empathy enables you to better understand and relate to your customer. Because you are able to connect and relate to them on a deeper level, you are able to communicate on a deeper, more emotional level and create messaging that resonates with them.

I feel empathy is no longer just an important skill for marketers but a must-have. It is needed for marketers to come up with a campaign, content, promotion and engagement activities that are relevant. Of course, we have access to insight but this is where empathy comes into play, to help you make effective assumptions. Performing empathy allows you to think and get into and understand your target customer's shoes and think about what they really care about and thus leverage the hot topics in your own brand's favour.

(Alice Yu Yuebo, Digital Content Lead, Prudential Assurance Company, Singapore, and Winner of The One to Watch, Women in Marketing Global Awards 2019)

If you don't bring yourself to work, you won't bring that empathy into work, and you then just miss out on some things which could be really obvious.

(Shweta Harit, Global Vice President of Marketing, Evian)[4]

TOP TIPS FOR DEVELOPING EMPATHY

- **Take time** to listen fully without distractions or second-guessing what the other person will say next – listen actively, and clear your head so you can be fully present
- **Define the role** the other person wants you to play and ask how you can help – for example, listen, coach or advise?
- **Don't be afraid to ask for more information** before offering advice – for example, ask how something feels or why it is important to the other person
- **Ensure the other person feels heard** and acknowledge how they are feeling – you don't have to agree, but this will help them feel heard
- **Build on your past experiences** – have you had a similar experience or felt the same emotion before? It doesn't have to have been exactly the same, but a similar experience will build empathy and help you relate to the other person's emotion

- **Reserve judgement** – if there is something that is stopping you from being able to do this, you may not be the right person to listen, coach or advise this individual in this situation, as you may be unable to relate to their situation or have any level of empathy
- **Practise** your empathy in a variety of different situations and with different people – can you imagine a situation from a variety of different people's perspectives? Someone on TV? A friend? A neighbour? Strangers?

QUESTIONS TO ASK YOURSELF
TO IMPROVE YOUR EMPATHY

- When someone shares a situation with you, are you willing and/ or able to see it from their perspective?
- Do you make the time to listen and understand?
- Can you relate to the situation? Can you draw on your own personal experience of a similar situation? (Your experience doesn't have to have been exactly the same.)
- Can you understand how they are feeling?
- Can you physically feel the same emotions they are feeling?
- How will you use this perspective to allow you to respond to your colleagues?
- How will you use this perspective to better connect with your consumers/customers?

CREATIVITY

WHAT IS CREATIVITY?

Creativity is the use of imagination, original ideas or inventiveness to create something. It can also be defined as "the process of having original ideas that have value."[5]

Let's break this quote down.

If we think of creativity as a **process**, then it must be something we can manage – personally and for our team.

Of course, **original ideas** are what we all strive for, but originality is all about context – what's original in one space may not be in another. There are many examples where the principles of a powerful idea in one sector have been applied to create something powerful and original in a completely different sector – think the ball-point pen influencing the (then) revolutionary roll-on deodorant!

Remember that **value** is about how we measure the success of an idea – obviously critical within our commercially focused marketing world.

WHY IS IT IMPORTANT?

Creativity is not just found among artists, graphic designers, writers and painters, and in marketing it is not just applied in creating advertising ideas or artwork design. It is a skill that allows you to solve a whole host of problems and make the most of opportunities. As it's a skill, it's something you can learn and improve on over time.

Creativity really is about understanding the world around us and seeing connections. So, I think somebody who is really creative is constantly curious. They constantly want to find out new things and are delighted by the things that they discover.

(Meredith O'Shaughnessy, CEO and Wizard, Meredith Collective)[6]

What's happened is people have lost the time or the ability or the desire to just wander a bit.

(Anthony 'Tas' Tasgal, Founder and Director, POV Strategy and Training)[7]

Creative thinking is not a talent; it is a skill that can be learned. It empowers people by adding strength to their natural abilities which improves teamwork, productivity and, where appropriate, profits.

(Edward de Bono)[8]

SHARE TIME

Creativity used to be one of my limiting beliefs (there is more on what this means in *Chapter 14*). I used to say "I'm not very creative," as my definition and beliefs about creativity were limited to artistic application. However, when I began to see creativity as a skill to problem solve, which I am great at, I started to take the time to adopt some of the principles in this section. As a result, my creativity (or problem-solving skill) has improved.

Curiosity and stimulus are the two key elements required to improve your creativity:

- **Curiosity**: this is interlinked with creativity and is the skill of asking why and understanding more (see earlier in this chapter for more on curiosity)
- **Stimulus**: I often say that we are only as good as our last stimulus. What are you doing to ensure your mind is exposed to as many different drivers and forms of stimulation as possible (just like with curiosity, as outlined above)?

The most exciting part of the creative process for me are those times when an individual or team makes a leap outside their everyday instinctive thinking – those relatively rare 'aha' moments when they gain a fresh perspective that can lead to diverse new and valuable ideas.

(Shelford Chandler, Creativity Consultant, Labyrinth Marketing)[9]

Creativity involves breaking out of established patterns in order to look at things in a different way.

(Edward de Bono)[10]

WHAT GOOD LOOKS LIKE

- You use creativity to develop propositions that satisfy the wants and needs of the customer, profitably
- You develop creative messaging and approaches to disrupt customer behaviour
- You use creativity to develop processes and approaches that solve internal challenges and improve the consumer/customer experience
- The ideas you generate are relevant – focused on solving a specific problem (i.e. a pain or gain point)
- The ideas you generate are unique, solving the problem in a way that surpasses your competition's or your own propositions
- Your ideas are based on human insight (see *Chapter 7*) – data is used to define the brief and build insight, but ideas cannot be automated and must be created by humans for humans

---

QUESTIONS TO ASK YOURSELF
TO IMPROVE YOUR CREATIVITY

- What can you do to gain a fresh stimulus? (Different journey to work, different experiences, new material, etc.)

- Where can you go to immerse yourself in your consumer/customers' world?
- What media can you absorb to stretch your thinking?
- What media are your consumers/customers watching that you can immerse yourself in?
- What can you do to adopt creative habits and behaviours?
- What creative thinking tools and techniques could you use?

THINKING BROADLY ABOUT YOUR COMPETITION AND MACRO TRENDS

WHAT DOES IT MEAN TO THINK BROAD?

Thinking broadly means covering a large number and wide scope of subjects. In marketing, it involves thinking about macro trends and what your competitors are doing, especially those outside your immediate category. Customers don't just see your category or organization – they have a wide view of the many other brands and businesses within their purchasing power.

I'd love marketing people to spend a bit more time wandering and looking at other areas which are beyond their comfort zone and certainly looking outside their market. If you work in cars or you work in yoga or you work in retail, you cannot spend all your working life just looking at your own market – you'll never come up with anything innovative or insightful or inspirational.

(Anthony 'Tas' Tasgal, Founder and Director, POV Strategy and Training)[11]

SHARE TIME

I review many brand plans, and what I often find is that their view of their customer landscape is narrow. The plans define their market only as the category in which they immediately operate, or they follow the definition of their market data source. Don't get me wrong – this is important to ensure you understand your direct competition and are monitoring your performance against these key players. However, you need to think more broadly. Who is your competition as your consumer/customer defines it? What else might they buy, instead of your proposition, to serve the same need? What might they buy as a result of a different need?

WHY IS IT IMPORTANT?

Thinking too narrowly means that you might miss out on an external macro, market or customer trend or opportunity that you could leverage. It could also mean that you are blindsided by competition from outside your category, affecting your performance and the speed with which you can react. Having a broader understanding of what's in your customers' sphere of vision can also help you to better communicate with your customers by considering a broader competitive set.

WHAT GOOD LOOKS LIKE

- You have identified macro trends that can be leveraged by your brand or business to help it grow
- Your competitor analysis isn't just based on those in your immediate category
- You conduct competitor scenario planning that looks at things from your competitors' perspective and understands their reasoning

---

QUESTIONS TO ASK YOURSELF
TO HELP YOU THINK MORE BROADLY

- What brands and businesses do your consumers/customers consider (inside and outside your category) that could address their pain or gain points?
- What else are you competing for other than money?
- Which of the current and predicted macro trends could you leverage?

BEING THE VOICE OF
THE CUSTOMER

WHAT DOES IT MEAN TO BE
THE VOICE OF THE CUSTOMER?

Being the voice of the customer means influencing others to act with the customer's interests at heart, ensuring that all decisions and activities implemented are to address a pain or gain point based on insight.

WHY IS IT IMPORTANT?

Marketing's role is to identify and satisfy the wants and needs of the customer, profitably. In order to do this, customers' needs must be at the heart of everything we do.

It takes time for an organization to change its orientations, especially other functions that may not be as close to customer insight as you or the marketing team are. Formally sharing insight into the customer's voice is the first step. This must be done in a way that is easy to understand and absorb, with clear actions on how to embed the voice (storytelling if you will – see *Chapter 9*) across the functions. This will help the whole organization to keep the customer's voice at the forefront in everyday meetings and decisions.

WHAT GOOD LOOKS LIKE

- You use personas to bring your customer's insight and voice to life
- These personas are shared across the whole organization and among key stakeholders to act as a constant reminder in day-to-day work
- You speak up in all forums and on all platforms to give feedback on whether ideas and practices resonate with your customer's voice

QUESTIONS TO ASK YOURSELF TO HELP YOU BE THE VOICE OF THE CUSTOMER

- What are the key wants and needs of my customers that I want the whole organization to be aware of?
- What forums, meetings and so on do I attend where I can ensure the voice of the customer is heard?
- Has any recent research been commissioned internally on the customer's voice? Can I cascade the key findings to the wider organization?
- What is the most effective way for me to deliver this to reach the relevant teams and ensure the key messages land?

CAPTURE TIME: KEY DISCOVERIES

1.

2.

3.

WHAT THREE THINGS ARE YOU GOING TO DO TO IMPROVE?

1.

2.

3.

CHAPTER SUMMARY

In this chapter, we reviewed the key human skills and thinking we need to develop to get into the hearts and minds of our consumers/customers. We also looked at the importance of being the voice of the consumer/customer in order to share this understanding. In the next chapter, we will look at the keys skills involved in bringing plans to life and motivating others.

CHAPTER 9

SKILLS TO LEAD AND MOTIVATE THE BUSINESS AND TO BRING PLANS TO LIFE

In this chapter we will look at the skills and behaviours we need to inspire and motivate ourselves and others to get behind the vision of the organization, brand, project or campaign. We will also examine the skills and behaviours required to deliver this vision into the business through enacting plans.

> *Nobody really tells you that what you learn in university, at business school and on courses – the technical part of marketing – is just your entry ticket. Then it's all about influence.*
>
> **(Thomas Barta, Founder, The Marketing Leadership Masterclass)[12]**

We will start by looking at leadership and management skills that can aid you as a marketer to lead the brand, the business and wider cross-functional teams – being a visionary, inspiring others, storytelling, taking ownership and providing commitment, being human, and being entrepreneurial. Leadership skills are now essential in marketing and not just for senior executives and board-level roles but across the function, as we need to lead from the front and drive change. We must marry up the goals and vision of the organization with the needs of the consumer/customer. Marketing is, or will soon be, the lead function that the organization leans on to deliver commercial growth.

We will then look at the skills required to motivate yourself and the organization to bring plans to life – bravery, conviction, resilience and a can-do attitude. Market conditions, customers, the competitive landscape, and internal people, processes and structures won't sit still and wait for us. Therefore, we need to continually drive forward and pivot where required.

VISIONARY

WHAT DOES IT MEAN TO BE A VISIONARY?

Being a visionary means dreaming big and seeing and feeling where you can take the brand, business or organization. It also means understanding that it takes time for others to see things this way and believe in it too.

WHY IS IT IMPORTANT?

As I keep emphasizing, marketing is the function that leads (or will soon lead) the commercial agenda of the organization. As such, marketing either leads change or aspires to lead change. A visionary is able to envisage and develop a view of the long-term future of the organization's customers and trends, and of the markets that the organization can leverage or operate within. They can also envisage how the organization will respond and be structured as a result. They almost sense where they should take the organization, based on a deep level of insight, as they can see the way forward using their intelligence and intuition.

I think to lead you have to have such clarity on the vision that you can take people on a journey with you ... I think sometimes leaders think they've done the job if they've set out a vision or expectation at the beginning, but there needs to be a continual reminder and what I call a 'label' and a link back to it. So, you need to really make sure that consistency is in place because that is how you change people's attitudes and behaviours – by continually reinforcing it.

(Katherine Whitton, Global CMO, Specsavers)[13]

Your ideas are only as good as your ability to make them happen, which for many marketers can become kind of a shock because you think you have all the skills ... Leading marketing is a 360-degree job.

(Thomas Barta, Founder, The Marketing Leadership Masterclass)[14]

WHAT GOOD LOOKS LIKE

- You can dream big and see a stretching yet realistic picture of what the business or brand can become and the benefits of it
- You are able to create a vivid image of this destination in your own mind and share what it will look, feel and be like – so much so that it becomes almost palpable
- You are able to translate that vision into clear goals or SMART objectives and milestones (see *Chapter 3*) – you dream big but realistically, mapping a path that validates for others that the goal is achievable
- You are able to use this vision to motivate and align teams to drive forward to achieve
- You use the principles of storytelling (see later in this chapter) to align the wider organization
- The vision is embedded in the organization's daily decision-making and communications, and it is regularly referenced in all forums
- You support your people and allow them the time to understand what the vision means for them personally

QUESTIONS TO ASK YOURSELF

- Have you taken time out to dream big?
- As well as doing this alone, have you taken time out from the day-to-day to do this with your team?
- What is your vision? For your organization? Business? Brand? Team? Yourself?
- Can you see and feel it?
- What will the benefits be of delivering the vision?
- What will your organization need to do to make the vision a reality?
- What will be the key milestones, objectives and goals that will enable you to achieve the vision?

- Have you shared your vision with your immediate team? Are they aligned? Did you they have any concerns or suggestions that you should take into account?
- How will you share the vision to inspire others in the wider organization?
- How can you bring the vision to life so they can see it and feel it, and become motivated to deliver it?
- What will you say and to whom? When, where and how will you say it?
- How will you deliver the message in a way that is fuelled by insight and emotion?

INSPIRATIONAL

WHAT DOES IT MEAN TO BE INSPIRATIONAL?

Being inspirational involves making someone feel that they want to, or can do, something. It allows others to see and feel your vision – so palpably that they want to be part of the journey.

It involves moving something ordinary into the realm of the extraordinary. It means being an example of how, with drive and passion, your organization can achieve greatness that wasn't there before.

Be the change you want to see. Go first. Simon Sinek says that "leaders eat last,"[15] but I think they need to go first. Your people should do what you do, not what you tell them to do. Show by doing, so they can follow your example. Show them what is possible.

WHY IS IT IMPORTANT?

The first step is to dream your end goal or destination. The next is to gain the belief and motivation of others around you. This is key, whether you are leading a radical change or transformation project for the organization, or providing day-to-day inspiration for your team and colleagues across the various functions.

> *If you don't know how to influence, it's very hard to do any good marketing. Very early on, learn how to build influence so all the great ideas you have actually have a chance to make it.*

> *What [my colleagues and I] found when we did a massive research project on the success of marketers is that, first of all, influencing skills matter more than marketing skills. In fact, they were over 55% of what matters, so the first step is realizing this.*

> **(Thomas Barta, Founder, The Marketing Leadership Masterclass)[16]**

I once asked a variety of marketers which line managers or leaders had stood out to them throughout their careers to date. They reported back that those who had stood out were those they had found to be inspirational – those who had achieved something or had overcome a challenge. But the important thing was not what they had achieved but how they had gone about it.

> *If your actions inspire others to dream more, learn more and become more, then you are a leader.*

> **(widely attributed to John Quincy Adams)**

There are many stakeholders that we need to influence and manage to bring strategies, plans and activities to market, whether that be internally (e.g. line managers, colleagues, other functions, boards and shareholders) or externally (e.g. trade bodies, unions, investors and the public). This is a key skill in leadership. Gaining alignment and buy-in from all stakeholders is a tricky but central part of our role as marketers. Although in this book I don't go into detail about how to address each stakeholder group, I do focus on agency partners (see *Chapter 5*), as this relationship is purely managed by the marketing function.

SHARE TIME

One organization I used to work for called the process of alignment 'socializing the plan,' meaning sitting down with everyone from whom you need buy-in ahead of a forum, board session or meeting so no one is put on the spot. This will mean they are also more likely to support you, so the project can move forward. Explaining the journey to date will validate your thinking and allow others to understand where you are going and why.

Acknowledging the change required is key, especially in discussions with anyone who is going to need to deliver the plan. Charging on ahead without acknowledging the importance of having alignment and motivation will, in my experience, lead to repercussions later and cause tension and conflicts across functions.

> *Don't be scared by the naysayers. Instead, say, "Oh, I hear you've got some different views on this. Tell me – I'm really interested in understanding your point of view."*
>
> **(Anthony Fletcher, CEO, Graze.com)**[17]

WHAT GOOD LOOKS LIKE

- You acknowledge that alignment is part of the journey of inspiration and you schedule time to do this in any process
- You share what you are doing and why you are doing it, so as to upskill those around you and provide transparency and understanding

- You understand and acknowledge that you need to gain buy-in from everyone in the wider organization and external stakeholders, to take them on the journey

---

QUESTIONS TO ASK YOURSELF

- Are you building a plan and long-term strategy with a cross-functional team so everyone is part of the journey from the start and becomes your advocate?
- Are you aligning others with the vision or plan after it has been developed?
- Are you including all relevant stakeholders? Are you clear on who needs to know what? And when, where and how they should be informed?
- Are you acknowledging those who are opposed to a proposed change? Are you taking the time to ask them about their views, showing them your interest in understanding their views in a non-confrontational way and in a private, safe space?
- Are you open to changing your perspective or approach if somebody gives you feedback you haven't previously considered?
- Are you considering the role of storytelling (see below) in everything you do?

STORYTELLING

WHAT IS STORYTELLING?

Storytelling involves using stories as a tool to help others in the organization to relate to a context or challenge that the organization is facing or a direction it is taking. It is about creating relatable and memorable messages.

In marketing, the concept of storytelling was initially used to launch products externally. Stories were created to show why a product had been developed and its role and purpose. This approach was made famous by the likes of Steve Jobs with Apple products.

However, storytelling is now increasingly being used as an internal alignment tool. It is a way to build internal clarity and resonance around upcoming and future activities, allowing us to move from PowerPoint decks filled with statistics and factual evidence to a story that is developed with emotion (and supported by the key statistics).

Storytelling uses insights (see *Chapter 7*) into how people feel or want to feel, what they need and want to know, and the best method to deliver it. It involves giving a balanced view of the key facts and emotion in order to disrupt, create resonance and land your key messages.

There is often a 'golden thread' or link throughout the story. The golden thread is the key message, take-away, pivotal question or viewpoint that you want to convey. It should be powerful and connect your story together. You can use evidence and statistics to support your golden thread, but be ruthless and only include statistics that are truly relevant.

Anthony 'Tas' Tasgal, expert in all things storytelling and author of *The Storytelling Book*,[18] has shared the following perspective:

> I worry now that in our industry, particularly in marketing comms, branding and sales, the pendulum has swung so far towards information, charts, bullet points, infographics and large amounts of numbers that we've forgotten the essential essence of communication, which is actually involving people emotionally, to get them to listen. Getting them to remember and feel emotionally attached to you.
>
> (Anthony 'Tas' Tasgal, Founder and Director, POV Strategy and Training)[19]

WHY IS IT IMPORTANT?

Storytelling is a great tool for engaging with internal and external audiences alike. It allows audiences to connect and relate with brands and businesses in a way that a simple message applied across multiple platforms just can't compete.

> *Storytelling is about how to make people care. [It is about] creating a relationship, a connection with readers, viewers or an audience, and using that for brands in a way that doesn't make them just look like they are pumping out messages in a very transactional way.*
>
> **(Anthony 'Tas' Tasgal, Founder and Director, POV Strategy and Training)[20]**

The great stories, with their isolated subjects, show us how to use the idea of the golden thread. If you explore your subject in depth, you will find a golden thread that can act as a source of unity, clarity, meaning and power in your story and your work.

Storytelling helps us relate to and care about what is about to happen. It moves people from seeing what is happening to having feelings about what is happening. It makes them feel involved.

> *People will forget what you said, people will forget what you did, but people will never forget how you made them feel.*
>
> **(widely attributed to Maya Angelou)**

Defining how you want your audience to feel before starting to create your story can help you to define your message and decide how to communicate it. Then develop your story to deliver that emotion.

If you're writing a presentation, doing a speech or creating a document, write down the emotional objectives of what you're trying to do.

(Anthony 'Tas' Tasgal, Founder and Director, POV Strategy and Training)[21]

WHAT GOOD LOOKS LIKE

- The story is considered at the start, during data collection and at the end of the process
- The desired emotion and key messages are identified at the start
- The audience and their preferred learning style are considered

QUESTIONS TO ASK YOURSELF

- Inspiration is contagious and it starts with you, so where does your inspiration come from? Who inspires you? Why?
- What have you done already that might inspire others to do the same?
- What did you have to do to achieve this?
- What can you do that will inspire and motivate those around you to believe and feel that they want to do the same thing?
- What have you achieved in challenging circumstances that others can relate to and draw inspiration from?
- Who do you need to inspire?
- How will you do this?
- What will you tell them?
- Is this a mix of rationality and emotion?
- Have all learning styles been considered? (covered also in *Unit 3, Chapter 1*)
- How could you use the storytelling method to help you build internal and external resonance?

OWNERSHIP AND COMMITMENT

WHAT ARE OWNERSHIP AND COMMITMENT?

Ownership involves leading from the front and taking responsibility for an idea or problem.

Commitment means being dedicated to a cause or activity. It often involves making a declaration about what you will do.

Think of yourself as the guardian (a bit like a parent) of the brand or business in your care. Put your arms around it, take responsibility and think about its long-term future – what areas of strength can be leveraged now and in the future? Define and help to build confidence in these areas of development. Spend time and resources nurturing the brand or business's strengths and areas of development to benefit its long-term growth and protect it from competitors.

I have personally always loved to work on brands that need to be turned around. Not brands that are ticking over but those that have lost their way, have had bad previous guardianship or have not had their equity maximized. It requires ownership and commitment to make a success of such brands.

WHY ARE THEY IMPORTANT?

In order to lead something, we must own it. We must take full responsibility and accountability for our role in the brand's or organization's growth, decline or turnaround. This doesn't mean just occasionally putting your hand up – it means remaining in a position of leadership and accountability even when the shit hits the fan. This means seizing the opportunity to own and lead, at all costs and in all weathers.

If, as a marketer, you are given or take an opportunity to lead, then use this golden opportunity for you and for the profession to show what greatness can be achieved when a marketer leads, puts their arms around a situation and owns the challenge. Provide commitment to lead and deliver by making a verbal external declaration to show your personal dedication to the task, so that others feel belief and motivation and hold you to account.

> *Commitment is where we get into action, where we declare what we stand for, where we're going and what we're going to do and what we're going to bring into existence. And, further than that, we invite others to hold us to account. A commitment does not stop until it's complete.*
>
> **(Peter Docker, Co-founder, Why Not Un Limited)[22]**

WHAT GOOD LOOKS LIKE

- You have defined a clear challenge
- Personal commitment is made verbally and externally about what you will do to grow the brand or business
- You take daily actions to deliver against this commitment

QUESTIONS TO ASK YOURSELF

- What is your current area of responsibility and ownership?
- What are you responsible for and what are you accountable for?
- What can you own and lead?
- What do you want to own and lead? What do you want to put your arms around?
- How will you approach taking the reins?
- What declaration of commitment will you make and how? To whom?
- Where is the brand or business now and where will you take it to under your ownership? What legacy will you leave behind?

BEING HUMAN

WHAT DOES IT MEAN TO BE HUMAN?

Being human means being authentic, honest and your true self. Connections and relationships are built between humans during moments of vulnerability and openness. If you want to connect with your team, so they trust and respect you, then being authentic and true will help you to form strong relationships.

WHY IS IT IMPORTANT?

Most marketers desire their leader to be inspirational (discussed above) but also human – someone who has empathy and is authentic and relatable. Showing you are human too, by being honest and vulnerable when needed, can really help to build connections and loyalty, as can having the emotional intelligence to notice when your team members or colleagues need extra support or are not aligned.

WHAT GOOD LOOKS LIKE

- Communications are honest and acknowledge true emotions (e.g. "Yes, trading is really tough right now and I am also feeling the pressure for us to perform")
- You admit when you have made mistakes and apologize
- You admit when you don't know the answer
- You are able to read your team members' body language and actions so you understand when they are not aligned or are demotivated
- Your team members truly feel understood

QUESTIONS TO ASK YOURSELF

- Do you share your authentic self?
- Do you praise others?
- Are you honest?
- Do you apologize?
- Do you empathize (see *Chapter 8*)?
- Do you share your weaknesses and challenges?
- Do you help?

ENTREPRENEURIAL

WHAT DOES IT MEAN TO BE ENTREPRENEURIAL?

Being entrepreneurial means being able to identify and leverage new strategic opportunities and then solving them creatively and quickly with fresh ideas and action. It involves taking risks (that others would avoid) in search of significant gain and celebrating so-called failures as learning and growing experiences.

Those with an entrepreneurial mindset often have strong strategic goals, are able to dream big, are creative, and have the drive and tenacity to make things happen.

WHY IS IT IMPORTANT?

We operate in saturated markets with a constant stream of new entrants and significant and increased customer demands, all in a digital age. The ability to identify a new prospect and quickly and bravely take action is key to carving out opportunities. It is the true sign of a test-and-learn culture.

A lot of people are working in start-ups and there's this desire to do an entrepreneurial type of work in a start-up or start your own business. Nothing stops you from acting like this where you are. Act like a founder – don't assume that just because you're in a large organization you don't have the room to do it.

(Shweta Harit, Global Vice President of Marketing, Evian)[23]

WHAT GOOD LOOKS LIKE

- There is curiosity to discover new opportunities or problems that need to be solved
- You have strong time-management skills, enabling you to bring ideas to market quickly
- You have a growth mindset (see *Chapter 15*)
- You are prepared and excited to leave your comfort zone to learn about markets, customers and business processes in an area you don't know anything about
- You have the resilience to deal with potential failures and are able to see that there's no such thing as a mistake as long as there is learning

QUESTIONS TO ASK YOURSELF

- Do you have the time to think strategically?
- Do you use creative approaches to your thinking to arrive at unique solutions?
- Have you previously identified an opportunity? Did you go after it or bring it to your business?
- If not, why not? What stopped you?
- Do you step out of your comfort zone? Are you willing to do so?
- Do you have the drive, passion and determination to make things happen?

BRAVERY

WHAT IS BRAVERY?

Bravery can be defined as having the mental or moral strength to face up to difficult or challenging circumstances or things of which we are afraid. Being brave means listening to your fearful voice and then stepping into the fear.

Chapter 15 delves deeper into the idea of stepping out of your comfort zone.

WHY IS IT IMPORTANT?

Without bravery, we are less likely to face challenges head on. We are also more likely to shy away from new market or growth opportunities due to a fear of not knowing how to address them or a fear of failure. Your brand or business growth depends on you being brave and moving forward, acknowledging the fear but working past it.

WHAT GOOD LOOKS LIKE

- You face into challenges to win in your market or with your consumers/customers
- You drive forward initiatives that aren't guaranteed to win and embrace that there may be a possibility of failure
- You continue to move forward even when you experience a fearful internal dialogue

---

QUESTIONS TO ASK YOURSELF

- If you knew you couldn't fail, what would you do?
- What growth opportunities have you avoided so far due to fear?
- What actions have you not taken due to fear of failure?

CONVICTION

WHAT IS CONVICTION?

Conviction is a strong belief or opinion and the drive to go after it. It often motivates others to join in. When a leader has personal conviction about a plan, they are far better able to lead their team and instil the same conviction in their employees.

WHY IS IT IMPORTANT?

Conviction provides you and those around you with the drive and appetite to make change. It provides clarity on where you will focus your activities and motivates those around you.

You need to demonstrate to others the conviction of your ideas. That can be anything from explaining something very clearly to putting some emotion into something, especially if it's a brand story or a grand vision, or rally cry, for people behind the organization. It means exciting people about going the extra mile to create something special.

So be clear, be analytical and set out your facts. But also put some fire into it. Talk about the importance to you as an individual of this thing. Certainly, I've been surprised in certain boardroom confrontations [at the effect it's had] when I've gone back to my personal convictions or really talked about how the consumer is going to feel about something.

(Anthony Fletcher, CEO, Graze.com)[24]

WHAT GOOD LOOKS LIKE

- Emotion is shared from the heart with personal experiences and beliefs
- People around you are excited and motivated to go the extra mile
- There is a balanced debate involving both analytics and feelings from the heart
- You are clear and believe in what you recommend should be done next, providing analytics to prove your point and emotion to help it land and motivate others
- You give your opinion (e.g. why you believe something is important for customers) and you represent the customer's voice (see *Chapter 8*)

QUESTIONS TO ASK YOURSELF

- Do you have belief and conviction in your current strategy or project?
- If not, what doubts do you have and how can you address them?
- Have you shared your conviction with your colleagues?
- Have you shared it with your team and the wider business?

RESILIENCE

WHAT IS RESILIENCE?

Resilience is the ability to bounce back quickly after a negative experience (e.g. shock, upset or loss). This is not to be confused with endurance, which is the ability to push through a negative situation but without making any progress in turning the situation around or making it more positive. Resilience means having the strength to turn around a challenge quickly.

WHY IS IT IMPORTANT?

As marketers, our markets, customers, internal structures and roles are forever changing. We need to have the resilience to pivot quickly from any given situation, whether an expected or unexpected change, either personal or professional. We must be able to quickly form a clear plan to turn around any situation, whenever the organization looks to us as if to say, "What now?"

> *The interesting thing about marketers is that they're responsible for the growth of a company. They're responsible for understanding and interaction with the customer. Looking at new growth strategies is an extremely important skill for everybody but particularly for marketers. But the reality is that all the clichés that we have around change are true. The only thing that's constant is change. You have to get comfortable with feeling uncomfortable.*
>
> **(Alice ter Haar, Founder, Badass Unicorn)**[25]

We are all human and of course we need to move through experiences at our own pace. We must give ourselves time to get over the shock and frustration of a situation and to work through any denial. However, it is important to be able to find the positives in a situation, using a positive mindset (see *Chapter 15*) to see and focus on the benefits, the lessons learned and possible solutions. When bad things happen, I often say to myself, "You have the day (or whatever is appropriate depending on the situation) to feel sorry for yourself and/or wallow under a blanket watching Netflix – and then tomorrow you will come back stronger."

It can be useful to refer to the Kübler-Ross change curve (also called the grief curve) to understand the phases you or members of your team may go through when a negative situation arises (see *Figure 9.1*). The change curve applies personally or professionally when you are looking to implement change or organizational change is happening.

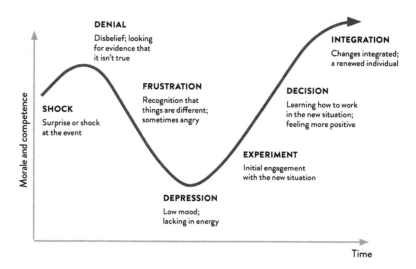

FIGURE 9.1 THE KÜBLER-ROSS CHANGE CURVE

The Wellbeing Project lists five pillars that are essential in ensuring you are resilient and helping to build your resilience levels:[26]

- **Energy**: mental and physical energy so you can withstand the weather and storms that come your way. This involves eating well, sleeping well and getting enough exercise. A healthy body and mind have a significant effect on our mindset and brain capacity.
- **Future focus**: a clear sense of purpose and direction to help you move forward. This comes from understanding your values and goals (see *Chapter 13*).
- **Inner drive**: the ability to sustain your self-belief and remain strong, confident and motivated.

- **Flexible thinking**: an open, positive and optimistic mindset. This involves making a decision about how you see a situation and not necessarily going down the victim route or letting your ego take over. It means really trying to take a step back and look at what is within and outside our control.
- **Strong relationships:** a good support network or 'board of advisers' who you can go to for advice or coaching when you need a different perspective or are facing a negative situation or challenge.

QUESTIONS TO ASK YOURSELF

Score yourself for each of the five pillars, from 1 (needs work) to 5 (strong):

- Energy: 1   2   3   4   5
- Future focus: 1   2   3   4   5
- Inner drive: 1   2   3   4   5
- Flexible thinking: 1   2   3   4   5
- Strong relationships: 1   2   3   4   5

Now consider the following:
- For which pillars did you score 3 or below?
- What can you do to improve on these pillars?

CAN-DO ATTITUDE
WHAT IS A CAN-DO ATTITUDE?

People who have a can-do attitude are positive, confident and resourceful in the face of a challenge or problem. They keep going and take action, and are willing to deal with problems or new tasks rather than complaining or giving up.

WHY IS IT IMPORTANT?

As mentioned previously in this chapter, our ability to pivot quickly, define a solution and action it is key. As with resilience, being able to bounce back in the face of a challenge is important, but so is dealing with new problems and tasks by taking action, positively. Of course, have a whinge, but dusting yourself off and keeping going is a skill in itself.

WHAT GOOD LOOKS LIKE

- You don't complain (for too long) and get on with what needs to be done
- You meet deadlines and help others around you to meet theirs
- You avoid things that might cause negativity, such as office politics
- You help others problem solve and come up with solutions
- You reward yourself and others for finishing tasks, especially the ones that were difficult and that you had to turn around

---

QUESTIONS TO ASK YOURSELF

- Do you have a can-do attitude?
- If not, why not?
- What can you do to improve how quickly you move from identifying a challenge to positively moving forward?
- How can you help your peers more and muck in when needed?
- What situations or conversations can you start avoiding to help you remain positive and not drain your energy?
- How can you reward yourself and others for delivering, especially when the going gets or has been tough?

CAPTURE TIME: KEY DISCOVERIES

1.

2.

3.

WHAT THREE THINGS ARE YOU GOING TO DO TO IMPROVE?

1.

2.

3.

CHAPTER SUMMARY

In this chapter, we looked at the key skills needed to motivate and inspire others, and to bring plans to life. These are also the key elements we need as leaders. In the next chapter, we will look more specifically at the skills required to be a respected and well followed marketing leader among your peers and team.

CHAPTER 10

LEADING THE MARKETING TEAM AND THE WIDER BUSINESS

WHAT IS A LEADER?

At the most basic level, leadership is about guiding and motivating a group of people to achieve a common goal or purpose. But a leader is more than that. For me, a leader is someone who has clarity on the vision, shares the vision and ensures their team is aligned behind it, truly cares, and thinks about the people they are responsible for as they would their family and friends.

To be completely honest, I used to think that either you were born a natural leader or you weren't. It was almost as if I thought a person could take one of the personality profiling tests mentioned in *Chapter 12* and if the test said they were a leader, they were – end of story. The problem with this approach is that it doesn't take account of the fact that marketing is the function that leads the business – in this light, the process just isn't going to work.

We need to think of leadership as an essential soft skill that is developed from day one of our marketers' careers. If you are a natural leader then great, but if not then it is a skill you can develop. Focus on building this skill as you rise through the ranks. You can start with leading work streams (e.g. analysis and reporting, campaign development, agencies or strategic planning). Then, you will be ready to exercise the skill when you gain more influence cross-functionally and become a part of leading the organization, its long-term growth and its commercial agenda.

Remember, leadership is not about dictating but about influencing and creating followership. This applies to everyone, in management and executive positions alike. The most important aspect of this skill is to remember that we are all human and want to be understood and appreciated, thought of as individuals, and feel motivated.

So, this chapter is here to acknowledge the importance of leadership as a soft skill in marketing that needs to be developed. We will examine what your colleagues and team want and need from you as a leader, and you will get a chance to reflect on the type of leader you want to be.

WHAT DO PEOPLE WANT IN A LEADER?

For me, a leader is someone who has clarity on the vision, shares and aligns this with their team, and truly cares and thinks about the people they are responsible for, as they would their family and friends.

Customers buy the people behind the brand, and your reports and colleagues buy you. They say that people never leave a job – they leave a manager. I have asked marketers what they are looking for from their leaders, and gone are the days when leaders could be dictatorial and simply set tasks and expect them to be delivered without question. Organizations are always changing, and supporting and leading people through change is a key component. The voice of the employee – and in this case marketers – is more powerful than it has ever been.

Leadership is a really difficult skill. You have to get people to want to follow and/or want to work with you, and this is where relationship-building comes in because people are more likely to want to be led by someone they like.

(Gemma Butler, Marketing Director, CIM)[27]

People are looking for leaders to be and do the following:
- **Personality**: be approachable, open, honest, authentic, empathetic (see *Chapter 8*), trustworthy and collaborative – do what is right
- **Motivate** through being a visionary and providing

inspiration (see *Chapter 9*), show gratitude and recognition for the work and commitment that people deliver, and treat people as humans and individuals

- **Provide support** as a mentor, coach, trainer and developer (see *Chapter 11*)
- **Provide clarity** on people's roles, direction, development plans, ways of working and expectations, especially through times of change – our roles are constantly changing and providing support through these transitions is key (see *Chapter 11*)

It is not an easy task to deliver against all of the items on this list, at the same time taking the time and energy to dream up the vision, align others behind it, deliver on goals from day to day, attend endless meetings, provide clarity on the present and the future, and so on and so on.

This is especially the case if you are not getting the support you need from above you. It can be lonely at (or near) the top. What support and motivation do you need to lead effectively? Will this come from inside your organization or outside it? Who can you turn to – a coach or mentor? Who do you get your inspiration from? Putting this support in place is essential to ensuring you have the space to think and the energy to deliver and start a ripple effect of positivity down through your team.

AUDIT: HOW WELL DO YOU KNOW YOUR TEAM AND REPORTS?

- How well do you know your reports and employees as individuals?
- What personality types are they? (See *Chapter 12*.)
- What do they need from you?
- What is their preferred working style?
- What are their values? (See *Chapter 13*.)

- What are their drivers or motivators? (See *Chapter 13.*)
- What are their strengths?
- How well do you leverage their strengths and help them acknowledge these?
- What are their areas of development?
- How are you supporting them to close the gaps in their development?

Let's now take the time to think about you as the leader.

WHAT TYPE OF LEADER DO YOU WANT TO BE?

Leadership isn't management. You manage a production line or a process. Leadership isn't authority or seniority. Leadership is the purpose of creating followership.

(Katherine Whitton, Global CMO, Specsavers)[28]

The previous section outlined what employees (or marketers in this case) are looking for from their leaders. I would like you to take the time to think about what type of leader you are, would like to be or need to be.

SHARE TIME

I often find in my coaching that what marketing leaders find hardest is leadership, particularly when this involves gaining cross-functional alignment. As this isn't a skill we are necessarily taught, we tend to lead in a way that we have seen before (either in our line managers or in other leaders in the organization). Often, I find that this jars with the people I coach as they feel they are not acting according to their values. It can create internal conflict about not being themselves or not doing things their way. This is why I suggest you take the time to think about what type of leader you want to be.

There are many models of leadership styles. *Table 10.1* shows one model, which splits leadership styles into six types. Use it as food for thought as to what type of leader you want to be (or don't want to be).

	COMMANDING	PACESETTING	VISIONARY	AFFILIATIVE	DEMOCRATIC	COACHING
Leader's modus operandi	Demands immediate compliance	Sets high standards for performance	Mobilizes people toward a vision	Creates harmony and builds emotional bonds	Forges consensus through participation	Develops people for the future
The style in a phrase	"Do what I tell you"	"Do as I do now"	"Come with me"	"People come first"	"What do you think?"	"Try this"
Underlying emotional intelligence competencies	Drive to achieve, initiative, self-control	Conscientiousness, drive to achieve, initiative	Self-confidence, empathy, change catalyst	Empathy, building relationships, communication	Collaboration, learn leadership, communication	Developing others, empathy and self-awareness
When the style works best	In a crisis, to kick start a turnaround or deal with problem employees	To get quick results from a highly motivated and competent learn	When changes require a new vision, or when a clear direction is needed	To heal rifts in a team or to motivate people during stressful circumstances	To build buy-in or consensus, or to get input from valuable employees	To help an employee improve performance or develop long-term strengths
Overall impact on climate	Negative	Negative	Most strongly positive	Positive	Positive	Positive

TABLE 10.1 LEADERSHIP STYLES

Source: Daniel Goleman "Leadership that gets results" *Harvard Business Review* Mar-Apr 2000

SITUATIONAL LEADERSHIP

Developed by Paul Hersey and Ken Blanchard, situational leadership is the idea that the leadership style you choose should be based on the situation you are in. According to this approach, leaders flex their style to meet the needs of the different people they work with and to respond differently to different situations.[29]

Many leaders instinctively flex their style based on the situation. The model helps by allowing us to grade or rate each situation and thereby identify the level of directiveness or support that needs to be given (see *Figure 10.1*).

SUPPORTING S3		**COACHING** S2
For people with: high competence var. commitment		For people with: some competence some commitment
"Let's talk D3 decides"		"Let's talk leader decides"
Low directive and high supportive behaviour D3		High directive and high supportive behaviour D2
DELEGATING S4		**DIRECTING** S1
For people with: high competence high commitment		For people with: low competence high commitment
"D4 decides"		"Leader decides"
Low directive and low supportive behaviour D4		High directive and low supportive behaviour D1

Axis labels: High / Low — Supportive behaviour (vertical); Low ← Directive behaviour → High (horizontal)

FIGURE 10.1 THE SITUATIONAL LEADERSHIP MODEL

THE 12 POWERS

Another way of understanding what it takes to be a marketing leader can be found in Thomas Barta and Patrick Barwise's *The 12 Powers of a Marketing Leader*.[30] In this book, Barta and Barwise define the 12 powers that marketing leaders need to possess.[31]

Reassuringly for me, not only are Barta, Barwise and I aligned on the importance of marketing leading the business and the benefits this brings, but we also have many similarities in our thinking. Each of the 12 Powers is covered in this book, as shown in *Table 10.2*.

THE 12 POWERS OF A MARKETING LEADER	THE WHOLE MARKETER
Mobilize your boss	
Power 1: Tackle only big issues	Chapter 3
Power 2: Deliver returns, no matter what	Unit 1, especially Chapter 6
Power 3: Work only with the best	Chapter 5
Mobilize your colleagues	
Power 4: Hit the head and the heart	Chapter 9
Power 5: Walk the halls	Chapters 8 and 9
Power 6: You go first	Chapter 10
Mobilize your team	
Power 7: Get the mix right	Chapters 12 and 13
Power 8: Cover them in trust	Chapter 10
Power 9: Let the outcomes speak	Chapters 6, 10 and 11
Mobilize yourself	
Power 10: Fall in love with your world	Unit 1
Power 11: Know how you inspire	Chapter 8
Power 12: Aim higher	Units 1 and 3

TABLE 10.2 THE 12 POWERS AND HOW THEY MAP ONTO
THE SKILLS AND CONCEPTS IN THIS BOOK

SHARE TIME

I have always lived by the principle when managing teams that I would never ask my team to do something I wouldn't or couldn't do myself. What principles do you have for yourself as a leader?

QUESTIONS TO ASK YOURSELF:
WHAT TYPE OF LEADER DO YOU WANT TO BE?

- Which leaders inspire you?
- What about those leaders inspires you? What traits, values, strengths and behaviours do they possess?
- What does leadership mean to you?
- What type of leader would you say you are?
- What type of leader do you want to be or not want to be?
- How would you want to be described?
- What do you want to be known for?
- What impact would you like to make on those around you?
- If you want to change your leadership style, what changes will you need to make to allow this shift to happen?

QUESTIONS TO ASK YOURSELF:
WHAT TYPE OF LEADER DOES YOUR TEAM
OR ORGANIZATION NEED YOU TO BE?

- What kind of leader does your team need you to be?
- What level of support or direction do they need?
- What kind of leader does your organization need you to be?
- Do you flex your style? Are you happy to do so?
- Is there a conflict between the leader you want to be and are asked to be?
- If so, how might you go about resolving the conflict?
- What support do you need to resolve it?

CAPTURE TIME: KEY DISCOVERIES

1.

2.

3.

WHAT THREE THINGS ARE YOU GOING TO DO TO IMPROVE?

1.

2.

3.

CHAPTER SUMMARY

In this chapter, we looked at some tools and models around leadership. You had a chance to reflect and start to define the type of leader you need and want to be to motivate and inspire your team and those in your care. In the next chapter, we will look at the importance of providing clarity to motivate others through capability frameworks, work streams, and training and development.

CHAPTER 11

BUILDING A HIGH-PERFORMING AND MOTIVATED TEAM

In this chapter we will continue to look at how we lead and motivate our teams. However, the focus in this chapter will be on providing clarity for your function or team, as well as for them as individuals. We will look at how to do this through capability frameworks, training and development work streams, as well as how to develop and support your team and individuals to deliver against expectations.

SETTING THE VISION FOR TEAMS AND FUNCTIONS

Having defined the long-term vision and corporate goals of your organization (see *Chapter 2*), you will need to determine how these translate into a vision for your function. This involves identifying the skills and knowledge your team needs to deliver the organization's strategy.

This is where a capability framework broken down into specific competencies and skill levels is required. It provides clarity not only for your function as a whole but also for individuals, outlining what is expected of them in their current role and any future role they may want to progress into.

Here is an example:

- **Organizational vision**: to be the most recommended brand of dishwasher by the end of 2025
- **Corporate goal**: to reach £100 million net profit by the end of 2025
- **Marketing function vision**: develop and lead the strategic plans and delivery, to deliver an incremental £20 million net profit by entering into the dishwasher market and developing the propositions agreed separately

I look at the CMO roles that I've done, and what's been a really important thread is that each has had a very clear story behind the team. That story was about what the team was achieving in terms of results and performance, and also where's the team going now? What's the strategy that's driving that team? Has the team organized to deliver that strategy? And what are the risks, what are the issues, what are the opportunities for that team? Who are the agency partners they're working with? How are they driving cost efficiencies and improvements? How are they looking to make things better for their customers? All those things are part of that narrative.

It's about updating the narrative of the team, which is a key theme. So if I look at a presentation I gave in a strategy forum, the first slide was a reminder of marketing's core strategy and focus areas for the year. And this presentation was an update on those two areas. But I used it to frame [everything] together. [In this way, I provided] a broad narrative: the top six to eight things that we're focusing on as a team.

(Pete Markey, CMO, Boots UK)[32]

CAPABILITY FRAMEWORKS AND COMPETENCIES

A marketing capability framework is a framework of marketing competencies that specifies required levels of proficiency. It provides clarity on what good looks like for both the technical skills and the soft skills expected of an organization's marketers.

This is not to be confused with a 'marketing way,' which is different from a capability framework. This is the way in which marketing is conducted in your organization. It may outline how you approach investment, bring products to market, develop and roll out marketing activation, and so on. It provides consistency on approach but usually has been considered in light of the competitive landscape, with proven approaches.

HOW TO DEFINE A MARKETING CAPABILITY FRAMEWORK

Following are the three key phases (and steps within each) that I recommend you follow to develop a marketing capability framework. I would suggest that if you have a large department or team, you build your capability framework with the involvement of a cross-functional working team (according to the idea of 'with you and for you'). This will help with alignment and encourage support and advocacy in your teams.

Define the competencies

1. Develop a vision and goals for your marketing team, function or division. This should provide clarity for your team on their role and on what they need to do and deliver to achieve these goals and in turn the organization's corporate goals.
2. Identify the competencies and knowledge your team, function or division needs to possess and demonstrate to deliver its vision and goals.

GETTING STARTED WITH DEFINING COMPETENCIES

If you are thinking "Where do I start?" – especially if you are defining competencies from scratch – you can refer to the skills outlined throughout this book (particularly in *Chapter 1*) or refer to the Chartered Institute of Marketing's Professional Marketing Competencies.[33] You may also have some specific competencies that are related to the type of industry in which you operate – say, financial services policies or bid management. Remember when you outline the skills to specify not just what you need but also the way it must be done.

Example competency: develop long-term strategic plans, based on customer insight, harnessing cross-functional teams' inputs and alignment.

---

3. Having defined the competencies, you can next define the levels of proficiency required for each tier. The average number of tiers is five. An example set of tiers might be 'aware,' 'developing,' 'proficient,' 'advanced' and 'expert.' The number of levels will usually reflect the number of ranks you have across your functions – for example, from marketing assistant to director or CMO. You can then provide the required proficiency for each of these levels.

Define the infrastructure and roles

1. Define the infrastructure and reporting lines of the roles. Bear in mind that there should be clear paths of progression.
2. Use your competencies and tiers to build role profiles and/or job descriptions, as required. You can either update existing ones or create new ones.
3. Communicate the framework to your marketing function along with details of how it relates to the organization's and function's vision and goals. Assuming you have built the framework with input from the team, there should be no surprise or shocks; build with your team for your team.

I think my biggest challenge internally was to get the right structure for my own marketing department, which I've changed around a couple of times. I think every couple of years you have to reassess and look at the skill sets you have.

(Gemma Butler, Marketing Director, CIM)[34]

Bring it to life

1. Now you can bring the framework to life across all the touchpoints where competencies will be discussed and used, such as job descriptions, recruitment, personal development plans and reviews, and succession planning. It should not just be left on an intranet.
2. Ensure it can be accessed by all, so that it can be referred to at any time.

SKILLS GAPS

Define the development gaps

Having defined the skills needed in your capability framework, updated your role profiles and job descriptions, and ensured alignment across individual team members and the whole function, I suggest you look into any skills gaps the new framework may have revealed, both for your function and for individuals.

Conducting a capability audit of your team's skills against the new competencies is a great way to assess your marketers' abilities. Doing so will allow you to face up to the gaps you need to close for the function and individuals. It is important to position this exercise carefully, to avoid any uncertainties about job security. The focus should be on the upcoming investment to upskill the team.

Having conducted the audit, it is important to assess the findings and cluster the development areas for both the team as a whole and individuals.

Finally, share the findings – initially in aggregate with the whole team and then with individuals, personally, so that individuals don't feel like they are being singled out.

Address the gaps now and in the future

Closing the gaps you have identified is essential, both for the group and on an individual level. You can do this both formally and informally.

Formal ways of closing gaps include the following:

- Training – ideally practical trainer-led face-to-face or virtual training or a blend of online and in-person learning, to allow for questions and embedding knowledge
- Talks by internal personnel and invited speakers
- Mentoring – this can be internal or external, but it may have to be external if the required skill is not present at an expert level internally

Some informal means are:

- Webinars
- Networking
- Marketing Weeks and campaigns
- Books and audiobooks
- Podcasts, such as *The Whole Marketer*[35]
- Subscriptions to newsletters by leaders and experts in the field

Remember too that the situation will not remain static. As highlighted in *Unit 1*, marketers' roles have broadened, and technological and digital advancements and evolving understandings of how to interact with customers mean that change will continue. Therefore, you will need to work to continually close gaps and periodically review and update your capability framework.

TOP TIPS FOR ALIGNING COMPETENCIES

You can nominate experts for each competency within your organization. They can then help to ensure that the expectations for their respective competencies remain in line with industry standards. They can also act as mentors for those who have been identified as needing development in a particular area.

SHARE TIME

All too often, time and energy are given to developing a capability framework and making it beautiful and colour coded for roll-out, but much less time is given to how the framework will be embedded in the day-to-day work of the organization. It is important to spend time considering the processes the framework will feed into, how you will deliver and launch it, and the training and development plans required for the function and individuals to close gaps. This will ensure the competencies are brought to life through all relevant touchpoints.

TRAINING, LEARNING AND DEVELOPMENT

I am sure most of you have a personal development plan process for yourselves and your team, perhaps with objectives or goals set annually with mid-year reviews. The ratio 70:20:10 is commonly mentioned in connection with time spent on career development:

- 70% on the job
- 20% mentoring
- 10% formal training

Bear in mind, though, that if you are implementing a significant shift in your team's competencies, you may need to temporarily increase the amount of time spent on mentoring and formal training.

Following are some pieces of advice from top marketers on career development:

Formal training is only 10% of how people learn. Most people learn on the job by having conversations with colleagues or being shown how to do something. I think it's a real challenge to find the time when you're working in a profession that has such a broad remit, and that is moving so fast and is incredibly noisy, to find the time to actually develop yourself. And I think that is a huge challenge for marketers who want to move up and want progress throughout their career, especially given all of the broadened roles that we now have to take on as marketers.

(Gemma Butler, Marketing Director, CIM)[36]

Always be hungry to keep learning and learn more and don't ever feel you've reached the end of any learning journey. Keep wanting to know more about marketing as a discipline.

(Pete Markey, CMO, Boots UK)[37]

Invest in yourself, write your own development programme and execute on it. So get yourself some mentors, hire a coach, sign up for conferences and seminars, watch TED Talks, but diarize your learning time. You know, invest in yourself with the objective of being the best human being.

You can be the most inspirational leader. You can be the most exceptional marketer. You need to understand what legacy and shadow you're going to create in the world once you leave it.

(Sherilyn Shackell, Founder and CEO, The Marketing Academy)[38]

ENCOURAGE A LEARNING CULTURE

Incentivizing your team to share with one another can be really valuable. They can share both what they have learned internally through execution and what they have learned externally through attendance of any of the formal or informal sources of learning listed earlier in this chapter. It doesn't have to be laborious – for example, you can set up a WhatsApp group to enable the team to share in real time things they have seen when at conferences, when out and about, or even when at home. This helps to create a great learning culture and also assists with team-building.

A few further examples of ways to embed a learning culture include:

- Test and learn exercises
- Coffee/Lunch and Learn events (these have an extra lure!)
- Sharing learning via email

Incentivizing a learning culture is a great way to keep the momentum going, and you can even offer relevant prizes that aid learning. For example, you could offer a trip to an exhibition or conference in New York for the marketer who shares the most learnings on a certain topic in a set period of time, and then they can share their learnings on their return.

PROVIDE SUPPORT

Having provided a capability framework, you will also need to support your team to deliver from day to day. We all know that delivering a vision is always much harder than dreaming it up, as we come across many hurdles and curveballs, whether physical, mental or emotional. It is crucial to put in place time to listen, advise and work through solutions with others (and by yourself alone).

Coaching and mentoring are key ways of providing support:

- **Coaches** tend to help a person define what they want to achieve and do
- **Mentors** tend to advise on how to do it, as they are experts in the field or topic in which the mentee wants to grow

It is beneficial for line managers to seek training in developing their coaching and mentoring skills. You can set up coaching and mentoring schemes internally to enable individuals to get advice on how they could approach a certain situation or challenge. If you are acting as the coach or mentor, use questioning and provide the space to support the individual to arrive at the answer themselves. Regardless of the approach, the most important aspect is your time and support, to acknowledge that individuals are not alone and provide guidance.

> *At the heart of the thing always for me as a leader is that I want the people that work for me to succeed and do well. And actually, it's lovely following the threads of all the people, particularly my core leadership team, and seeing them all land in really great jobs in terms of what they're doing in the brands that they're working with now.*
>
> **(Pete Markey, CMO, Boots UK)[39]**

WAYS OF WORKING

It is invaluable to establish ways of working for your team and between you and your direct reports and agency partners. This allows you to get off to the right start by gaining a deeper understanding of each other, what you value and what you need to be motivated to deliver. In addition, it will enable you to understand practicalities about how best to work together, such as:

- Working patterns
- Preferred method of contact
- Preferred communication style
- When best to get hold of each other

WHAT GOOD LOOKS LIKE

- The leader is both visionary and inspirational but also approachable, human and authentic
- The leader makes time to support their people, cares about them as individuals, and has a good understanding of them as individuals and what they need to be effective and motivated
- The leader establishes clarity around goals and expectations through a capability framework, ways of working and regular meetings
- The capability framework is built to deliver against the function's vision and goals as well as industry standards, and is made accessible and applicable for each rank
- The leader ensures the capability framework is brought to life through all touchpoints so as to support delivery and future career development
- The leader ensures the capability framework is periodically reviewed, up to date and relevant
- The leader encourages a supportive working environment with a learning culture

QUESTIONS TO ASK YOURSELF

- What role do you want your marketing team or function to play in delivering the organization's vision and goals?
- Does your team have clarity on the organizational and team visions?
- Do they have clarity on what competencies they need to possess or deliver personally and for the organization?
- Do you understand what learning and development the function and individuals require to deliver and grow?
- How well do you know your reports and employees as individuals? What they need? Their values? Strengths? Areas of development?

- Do you have ways of working in place? Between individuals?
- Do you make yourself available to listen to, mentor or coach your team members?

CAPTURE TIME: KEY DISCOVERIES

1.

2.

3.

WHAT THREE THINGS ARE YOU GOING TO DO TO IMPROVE?

1.

2.

3.

CHAPTER SUMMARY

In this chapter, we looked at motivating your team and individuals by providing clarity on expected deliverables through a capability framework. We also examined how to support this framework through training, developing a learning culture, providing support through mentoring and coaching, and defining clear ways of working. All of these elements aim to support and empower the humans behind the brand or business.

In *Unit 3*, we will take a deeper look at you – who you are, your values, your purpose and what might be getting in your way. Once you understand these aspects of yourself, you can start to create a ripple effect by using the tools and principles in this unit to motivate those in your care at a deeper level.

UNIT 3

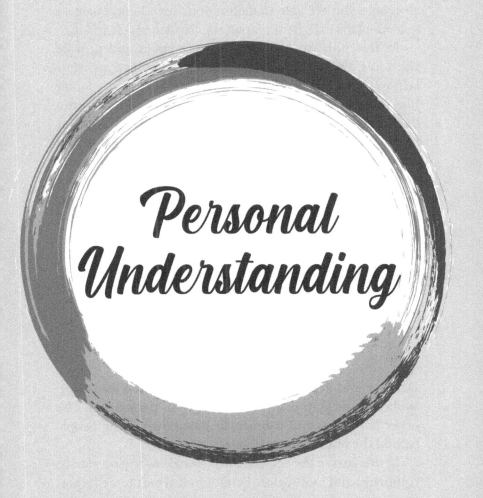

Personal Understanding

WHAT IS COVERED?

In *Unit 1* and *Unit 2*, we defined the technical skills and the soft and leadership skills you and your marketing team need to ensure you are able to deliver your brand and business growth plans in light of marketers' broadened role today.

In this unit we will look to understand and provide the tools and techniques to allow you to increase your self-awareness by defining who you are and what you are like to be around (personality), what motivates you on a deeper level (values and drivers), what brings you fulfilment (goals and purpose), what may be stopping you (beliefs and mindset) and principles you can use to bring plans and goals to life. Whereas *Unit 1* looked at the 'what' and *Unit 2* looked at the 'how,' this unit looks to your purpose and your 'why' – what makes you come alive in your heart and soul and why you get out of bed every day.

In short, this unit is all about *you* – who you are as a person, not as a marketing executive, marketing manager or head of marketing.

WHY IS THIS IMPORTANT?

Defining and developing the technical, soft and leadership skills you and your team need is only half the journey. The other half relates to the people themselves – the people behind the brands and businesses.

In this part of the book, we will cover how to gain clarity, fulfilment and motivation. What often seems to be forgotten is that we are all human and psychological barriers get in the way, such as "I'm not good at numbers," "I don't have the time" or "What if I fail?" This may be why some people struggle with certain projects or activities even when they technically know what to do.

Now is the time for you to work out what you want and define your goals for your life as a whole.

Your personal and professional lives need to be in harmony for you to feel like you are living your best life ... we bring our whole selves to work.

(Mary Portas)[1]

Who are you as a human? Getting to know yourself at a deeper level and defining your personal and professional goals will allow you to live your best life and have a fulfilling career in marketing.

If you don't understand what you're on the planet to achieve, what you're truly, deeply passionate about, what you're brilliant at, what your spikes are, what your areas are where you excel, then it doesn't matter how good your technical skills are – it's going to hold you back.

(Sherilyn Shackell, Founder and Global CEO, The Marketing Academy)[2]

This unit applies to everyone – marketer or not – and it may be something you want to revisit at different moments and crossroads throughout your life. You may also want to use these tools and concepts with your team members, to help you understand them and help them understand themselves better. You can only help others to the extent to which you know yourself.

Following are a few extra thoughts to consider as you go through this unit.

SELF-DISCOVERY IS WORTH YOUR TIME

Investing time in self-discovery is 100% worth it. I have personally been on a journey of self-discovery over the past few years. I was already fairly self-aware and knew what motivated me and didn't. However, taking the time to discover and gain a deeper understanding of myself – namely my goals, my values and my 'why' – has fundamentally changed my life. When I defined these for myself, I really felt as if I started to live my life to its fullest, as I was able to make decisions that would play to my values and move me toward personal fulfilment.

As part of a mission to deliver my purpose of helping others to grow, I have also invested the time, money and energy to become a qualified and accredited coach. So, the advice, tools and techniques I am about to give you come not only from my own experiences and learnings resulting from my own self-discovery but also from coaching courses and workshops I have attended as an accredited coach of the International Coaching Federation.

I encourage you to do the exercises in this unit and take the time to reflect. This will not only enlighten you but will also allow you to understand others you work and live with better. You will be able to build deeper connections and understanding of them, and help them to grow too. Your self-discovery and sharing will have a ripple effect on others around you.

GETTING IN THE RIGHT FRAME OF MIND

You are probably thinking, "Easier said than done – I'm always so busy."

I'm sure you are spending your working weeks delivering campaigns and product launches, attending forecasting meetings and leading strategic planning sessions – all alongside the demands of general life admin, school runs, social commitments and so on. Especially when the weekend arrives, all we want to do is relax, spend time with our friends and family, and do something that makes us feel alive.

So, before you embark on this unit, I encourage you to start believing that *you are worth the time*. We often give our family, children, friends and colleagues our time, but when was the last time you focused on you?

The most important project you will work on is you.

Especially for those who are looking after others as parents or carers, or managing a team, the oft-repeated oxygen mask analogy is true: you need to put the mask on yourself, so you can breathe, before you help anyone else. Remember, understanding yourself better will also help those around you.

CHAPTER 12

WHO YOU ARE: WHAT ARE YOU LIKE TO BE AROUND?

This chapter is designed to allow you to increase your self-awareness, own who you are and understand more about what you are like to be around. It will provide you with tools and techniques to help you gain a deeper understanding of you as a person and what drives and motivates you, as well as understand others in your team and who you work with.

In life, we are the lead character in our own story. If you don't understand, feel connected with or even at ease with the main character in a story, you are unlikely to enjoy the narrative to its fullest as it unfolds.

> *You either walk inside your story and own it or you stand outside your story and hustle for your worthiness.*
>
> (Brené Brown)[3]

Job titles only describe the role that we do while at work. This is the chapter that gives meaning to the 'whole' aspect in the title of this book, as we bring – or should bring – our whole selves to work and not forget about the person behind the job title.

WHY IS IT IMPORTANT TO UNDERSTAND YOURSELF?

Defining your personality will not only help to increase your own self-awareness but also enable you to communicate to others what you are like to be around and work with and how to get the best out of you. This will be relevant to how you interact with prospective employers (including through your CV and in interviews) and with your existing team (to define ways of working).

It will also allow you to improve your understanding of others in your team and motivate them individually on a deeper level. For example, you will be able to help John grow and develop, not just your product-marketing manager. Another benefit is that you will be better able to build effective teams and ways of working, and ensure that you are recruiting people with personality traits that complement and enhance your existing team.

Let's get started on defining your personality.

WHO ARE YOU?

What are you like to be around? What is your personality type?

It is wonderful to be loved, but it's profound to be understood.

(Ellen DeGeneres)[4]

In order to understand others, in all aspects of life including how you relate to your team and colleagues, you need to understand yourself first.

When you align your personality with your purpose no one can touch you.

(Oprah Winfrey)[5]

EXERCISE: SELF-AWARENESS AUDIT

In this exercise, aim to think about the whole of yourself – both work and personal life.

How well do you know yourself?

What kind of person are you like to be around?

How would you describe your personality?

How would others describe your personality?

Do you know the aspects of your personality that are positive?

Do you know the aspects of your personality you may need to be mindful of?

What are you like when you are at your best?

What are you like when you are at your worst?

Are you an introvert or extrovert?

Do you know your preferred learning style – in other words, how you best absorb information given to you? Is it:
- Written
- Verbal
- Visual
- Kinaesthetic (through doing it)
- Combination

How do you make decisions? Is it:
- With data, facts or statistics
- Logically
- By sensing what is right from feelings in your body (e.g. your heart or gut)
- From what you know is right or what you feel to be right
- From engaging in counsel from others
- Other

What motivates you?

What demotivates you?

Which personality traits do you value in others?

Which personality traits do you dislike in others?

EXERCISE: PARTY OF FIVE – FEEDBACK

This exercise allows you to get feedback from five people around you as to what you are like to be around from perspectives external to you.

Step 1

Decide who to ask. You can ask whoever you like, but I would recommend a mix of friends and colleagues, so you get a rounded view.

Step 2

Reach out: explain what you are doing and ask the individuals for their help. If they agree, provide them with the questions below, preferably via email, so they have time to reflect and reply more honestly than they would if you were face to face.

Name:
1. Which words or phrases describe me best?
2. What am I like to be around?
3. What do you think is my greatest achievement?
4. What do you value about me the most?
5. What is one thing that I could change or modify for my own benefit?
6. What do you believe to be my greatest strength?
7. Based on what you have seen of me in the past and how I am today, if you were to give me one piece of advice for the future, what would it be?

Step 3

Collate the responses and compare them with how you described yourself in the previous exercise. Do the responses reflect your view of yourself and your values (see *Chapter 13*)? Is there anything you weren't expecting? Did the responses raise anything that you weren't aware of?

Step 4

Own it: you are who you are. This is what makes you *you*. However, of course, you need to be mindful of how you interact with others to ensure that you are understood and that the interaction is a positive one, so if there is any feedback that you want to work on, think about how best you can do so.

By being you, you put something wonderful in the world that wasn't there before.

(widely attributed to Edwin Elliot)

PERSONALITY PROFILING TOOLS AND TYPES

Having an understanding of your personality type is useful. It helps you to understand the way you prefer to communicate and make decisions in the workplace, taking into account your views and preferences. There are many personality profiling tools available. My aim over the next few pages is to share with you some of the most common tools used within organizations to understand people and teams.

These tools can be useful as they are objective and can support you to build effective teams that have a mix of all personality types. They can also help you to improve communications within your team and between the team and other colleagues by understanding each person's personality, their communication and decision-making styles, and their preferences about sharing with others. This increased understanding will improve the effectiveness of your communications, gaining alignment and buy-in too.

That said, by their very nature these tools put us in boxes (usually one of 16). I would therefore say that they are useful as starting points but not definitive, because as humans we don't always fit into one box.

You don't have to complete each tool formally (although I have included links to the tools in case you wish to do so). You may wish to use aspects of the descriptions that most sound like you as prompts to help you describe to others who you are and what you are like to be around.

MYERS–BRIGGS TYPE INDICATOR

The Myers–Briggs Type Indicator (MBTI) assessment is based on 16 personality types developed by Katharine Cook Briggs and Isabel Briggs Myers.[6] They in turn built the personality types on the work of Carl Jung conducted in the early 1900s.

The MBTI takes the form of a questionnaire. After you have completed it, you receive a four-letter acronym that reflects one of the 16 personality types. *Table 12.1* lists the areas the MBTI examines and the associated letters.

AREA	LETTERS
How you interact with the world	E: Extrovert
	I: Introvert
How you absorb information	S: Sensor
	N: Intuitive
How you make decisions	T: Thinker
	F: Feeler
How you organize yourself	J: Judger
	P: Perceiver

TABLE 12.1 AREAS ASSESSED BY THE MYERS–BRIGGS TYPE INDICATOR

TAKE THE ASSESSMENT

You can find a list of the 16 profiles and options to conduct the assessment at www.myersbriggs.org.

CAPTURE TIME: THE MYERS–BRIGGS TYPE INDICATOR

1. What Myers–Briggs personality type are you? (I'm an ESTJ in case you're wondering.)

2. How could you use this information in your workplace?

3. Do the people around you have similar types or are they different?

INSIGHTS DISCOVERY

The Insights Discovery tool provides individuals with a colour profile to allow them to understand their personality type, how they make decisions and how they are likely to interact with others. It can help you to understand yourself, understand others and improve your relationships at work. Like the MBTI, it is based on psychometric questions, which originate in Carl Jung's thinking. It's often used when new teams are formed, when conflict is occurring or when change is afoot to help people understand each other better and build effective teams.

The findings are presented in a wheel made up of four colours, each representing a personality type (see *Figure 12.1*): Fiery Red, Sunshine Yellow, Earth Green or Cool Blue (or commonly just the colours red, yellow, green and blue).

The tool is a favourite among organizations due to its simple language, which can easily be used and understood within teams. It looks to determine how people may behave and advises how best to communicate with them.

You can be a mix of the colours – for example, I am red and green. The tool aims to show you the varying degrees of your personality, both naturally and when 'adapted' (e.g. under stress).

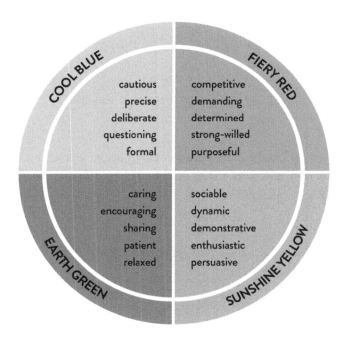

FIGURE 12.1 THE INSIGHTS DISCOVERY COLOUR WHEEL

In my opinion, the most useful part of this tool is that it tells you how best to communicate with people who correspond with each of the colours. I have found this to be a useful way of increasing my self-awareness and discovering how to get the best out of others and motivate them.

TAKE THE ASSESSMENT

You can find out your colour profile – or ask your team to do so – at www.insights.com/products/insights-discovery.

CAPTURE TIME: INSIGHTS DISCOVERY

1. What is your Insights Discovery colour profile?

2. What new insights did it provide you about yourself?

3. How will you use these insights moving forward?

4. Think of one or more colleagues with whom you work closely. For each one, what is their insight colour profile (or what do you think it would be)?

5. How will you change your approach to these colleagues moving forward?

EVERYTHING DiSC

Everything DiSC is a rigorously researched self-assessment tool that helps you to understand why you, and others, behave in the way you do in the workplace.[7] The four dimensions – Dominance, Influence, Steadiness and Conscientiousness – describe the typical behavioural styles of individuals.

DiSC assessments are used by individuals and teams to help them understand and develop their skills and capabilities, drive performance and bring about cultural change. They help people to develop their self-awareness and adaptability around behaviours, improve their working relationships, strengthen their management skills, elevate their leadership impact and tackle conflict with a new mindset. *Figure 12.2* shows the four dimensions.

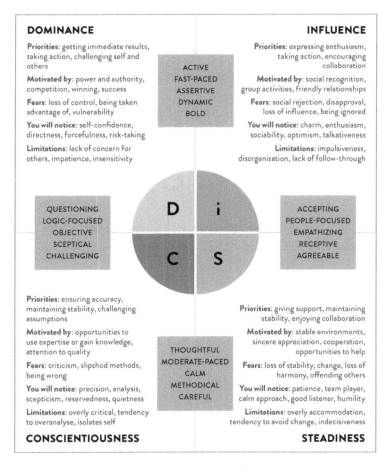

FIGURE 12.2 EVERYTHING DiSC

TAKE THE ASSESSMENT

To learn more about the range of Everything DiSC profiles and to complete an assessment, visit www.thefruitfulgroup.com.

CAPTURE TIME: EVERYTHING DISC

1. What's your DiSC personality type? (Mine, in case you're wondering, is i.)

2. What insights does your personality type provide about yourself?

3. How will you use these insights moving forward?

4. Think of one or more colleagues with whom you work closely. For each one, what is their DiSC personality type (or what do you think it would be)?

5. How will you change your approach to these colleagues moving forward based on this information?

PUTTING YOUR SELF-DISCOVERY INTO PRACTICE

Whether or not you choose to complete any of the personality profiling tools above, keep going deeper into understanding yourself. What drives you? What makes your soul happy? What makes you come alive? When do you feel the most fulfilled?

What I have found to be the most life changing is taking the time to understand my values and help others to define theirs too. When you understand yourself and your values, you really begin to unlock things within yourself (we will look more at values in the next chapter).

All of these tools are good for understanding your colleagues' personalities and how to interact with others to get the best out of each other. This is especially the case when you are building a new team or working in a team with a mix of personalities, as the tools can help you to ensure there is effective collaborative working. That said, keep in mind that the tools mainly highlight how people think and make decisions, not what makes their soul sing or drives them.

EXERCISE: WORKING BETTER WITH OTHERS

How well do you know others in your team?

Do you know how they like to be communicated with?

Do you know how they arrive at decisions?

Do you know how their mind best takes information on board?

How will you use this information to improve your communications?

How will you use it to gain alignment?

QUESTIONS TO ASK YOURSELF

Now that you've read this chapter and perhaps completed one or more of the assessments, think again about some of the questions asked earlier in the chapter. Have your answers changed? What new things have you learned?

- How well do you know yourself?
- What kind of person are you like to be around?
- How would you describe your personality?
- How would others describe your personality?
- Do you know the aspects of your personality that are positive?
- Do you know the aspects of your personality you may need to be mindful of?
- What are you like when you are at your best?
- What are you like when you are at your worst?

CAPTURE TIME: KEY DISCOVERIES

1.

2.

3.

**WHAT THREE THINGS ARE YOU
GOING TO DO NEXT?**

1.

2.

3.

CHAPTER SUMMARY

I hope that you have found this chapter thought provoking. Wherever you are on your journey of self-awareness, try to find the time to think about what makes you *you*, as well as how learning more about your colleagues will improve your ways of working.

So, having increased your self-awareness, explored your personality profiles and examined what you are like to be around, in *Chapter 13* we will look to define what drives and motivates you on a much deeper, soul level – your values and purpose.

YOUR VALUES: WHAT MOTIVATES YOU AND GIVES YOU PURPOSE?

In this chapter we will go deeper than just how we define our own and others' personalities. We will look at what brings you fulfilment and makes you come alive in your heart and soul (values) and why you get out of bed every day (purpose and why).

This chapter is designed to allow you to increase your self-awareness. It will also provide you with the tools and techniques to gain a deeper understanding of yourself as a person and what drives and motivates you – what makes you come to life and makes your soul sing.

WHAT ARE VALUES?

Values are the energy and motivation behind your goals. They are the things that you deem to be of high importance and that give meaning to your life. They are activities, behaviours, beliefs and qualities that matter to you and make your soul come to life.

Understanding your values will allow you to take action to spend time and energy doing things that allow you to live and breathe them. They are not *what* you do but *why* you do them. Ultimately, values are principles by which you want to live your life, professionally and personally.

THE BENEFITS OF DEFINING YOUR VALUES

Living your best life means doing things both personally and professionally that allow you to play to your values. Knowing your values brings the following benefits:

- **Easier decision-making**: in all aspects of your life (e.g. job, activities and goals), you can choose the options that are most closely aligned with your values

- **Increase in fulfilment and energy**: by choosing hobbies and interests that play to your values, you will gain fulfilment and energy from being at your best
- **Deeper self-awareness and understanding**: this will help you to understand why certain actions, people and situations fill you up and others bring you down or drain your energy
- **Ability to be more objective**: you will be able to look at unsatisfactory situations and relationships in a more reflective light
- **Better prioritization of your time**: you will better be able to gravitate toward doing things that allow you to serve your values – and, if you are having a bad day, it will be easier to identify something to do that will play to your values, to improve your mood
- **Better understanding of others**: we are more likely to get on with people who share our values – knowing what yours are can help you to understand why you connect with some people and don't gel with others
- **Ability to help others understand their values**: everyone's values are different – start with understanding your own values and then help others (personally or professionally) to identify theirs
- **Better ability to express your values to others**: if someone has annoyed or upset you, speaking from your values can allow you to give them better feedback (e.g. "When you said *x*, it made me feel *y* because I value *z*")

There are also specific benefits in the working world:
- **Better choice of roles, tasks and projects**: you can opt for areas that play to your values to ensure you feel fulfilled – or assign work to others that plays to theirs
- **Increased motivation**: this can result from communicating and acting in a way that your team and colleagues value (e.g. honestly or kindly)

- **Recruitment**: you can recruit people who have the values the organization strives to embody
- **Partners**: you can choose agency and other partners with similar values to those of your organization

Combining your values with your personality is where the magic happens.

(Oprah Winfrey)[8]

SHARE TIME

One of my values is to be open and honest, so here are my own values along with my own personal definitions and examples of how I ensure I live by them:

- **Openness and honesty**: being open and honest with others to help build a true connection with them, and also being open and honest with myself
- **Helping others**: giving back and having a positive effect on others
- **Connection**: connecting with others through my relationships and friendships with others, and having a mutual support network that allows me to have roots, keep building connections, and meet new people and understand them
- **Growth**: constantly learning and evolving
- **Generosity**: giving to others, whether it is my time or gifts that make others happy

---

QUESTIONS TO ASK YOURSELF

- What do you value in life and from others?
- Are you living your life in accordance with your values?
- Why do you get out of bed in the morning?

ENGAGING WITH YOUR VALUES

There are three levels at which we engage with our values:

1. **Identify** and define them
2. **Acknowledge** them and increase our awareness of how they affect us
3. **Embody** and share them with others; start defining and actioning activities that allow you to live by your values in your day-to-day life – this is where the magic really starts to happen

It's not hard to make a decision when you know what your values are.

(widely attributed to Roy Disney, older brother of Walt)

IDENTIFYING YOUR VALUES

It takes time to work out your values, but this time is invaluable as the knowledge you gain will soon become a checklist for decisions you make. If you are struggling with a situation, it's probably because it's not playing to your values.

Over the following pages, you will find various exercises to help you to identify your values. As you work through them, bear in mind that the following will help you through the process:

- **Time**: take yourself off somewhere quiet and away from your normal routine.
- **Clustering and a listener**: sometimes it's helpful to have someone to listen to you and help you cluster together themes in your thoughts. This can be a trusted friend, a colleague or a coach. My only caveat here is that you should pick someone who doesn't know you very well and who wasn't around during your childhood, as this kind of person may struggle to be objective. They need to hear what you are actually saying and not what they think or their version of what happened in your past.

- **Self-care**: having discussed your past, you may need some time to look after yourself. Doing a values session and then heading to an agency briefing may not be the best idea. Taking a walk or having a little nap may be kinder to yourself.

Starting to think about your values

There are many techniques available and questions you can ask to help you identify your values. Let's start with some questions.

EXERCISE: GETTING STARTED WITH VALUES

Answer the following questions with the first thoughts that come to your mind:

What brings you joy?

What are you passionate about?

What are you doing when you feel at your best?

What are you doing when you feel at your worst?

What do you value in others?

What do you dislike in others?

Are you seeing any common themes?

EXERCISE: YOUR KEY MOMENTS

Identify five or more key moments in your life (positive and negative).

What was happening?

What made these moments so significant?

Why were these moments important to you? (Try to focus not on each event but why it was significant to you, what you were gaining or losing. For example, if several of your key moments were spent with your friends and family, your value is not about being social – it's about what those occasions gave you, such as a sense of belonging or connection.)

Clustering and themes

You are probably starting to notice some overlaps between themes and scenarios that are starting to appear. The next step is to think about these overlaps and what they highlight about your values.

EXERCISE: NAME YOUR VALUES

Below I have listed some values that may be relevant to you or at least provoke your thinking. Using your answers to the exercises above and keeping in mind any overlaps you've noticed in themes, scenarios or words, circle any of the values below that stand out to you (or add your own).

Next, think about how you would define each of the values you have circled – what does each one mean to you? Then, in the space below, see whether you can narrow your list down to a few core values.

Don't worry if you don't arrive at your final list straight away – you may need to sit with your initial list for a while or spend some time refining it.

Courage	Creativity	Nature
Challenge	Winning	Wealth
Excitement	Freedom	Home
Acceptance	Self-respect	Honesty
Fulfilment	Passion	Friendship
Adventure	Wisdom	Peace
Integrity	Sensuality	Wellness
Loyalty	Leadership	Patience
Faith	Inner peace	Health
Consistency	Doing the right thing	Support
Achievement	Compassion	Independence
Recognition	Gratitude	Learning
Bravery	Service	Growth
Inner strength	Encouragement	Safety
Connection	Joy	Respect
Love	Dignity	Trust
Power	Happiness	Authenticity
Family	Spirituality	Sense of belonging
Fairness	Security	

Your values

1.

2.

3.

4.

5.

It is essential that you describe what each value means for you, as individuals' values may have the same title but different meanings. For example, two individuals might have 'faith' as a value but for one this might mean religious belief and for the other it might mean having faith in their actions and all they do.

Description 1:

Description 2:

Description 3:

Description 4:

Description 5:

Refining your values

I recommend that you share your drafted values and descriptions with trusted family, friends and colleagues to seek feedback and refinements. This will also be your first step in acknowledging them by sharing them either in writing or verbally (out loud).

You might also want to cross-reference your list of values with the feedback you gained from the Party of Five exercise in *Chapter 12*. Are there any similar themes? Do any of the Party of Five answers affect how you feel about your list of values?

ACKNOWLEDGING YOUR VALUES

Once you have defined your values, the next step is to acknowledge them. Acknowledging your values increases your awareness of them. By doing this, you can start to use your values to improve your understanding of current or past situations. Try the exercise below to explore why a past event jarred with your values.

EXERCISE: SENSE CHECK

Review a recent situation (different from any of the ones you have listed above) that annoyed or upset you. Using your new found knowledge of your values, describe why you felt this way.

EMBODYING YOUR VALUES

The final step is to embody your values in your day-to-day life. Think about the following:

- Who will you share your values with?
- How will you use them?
- Are there any decisions that you need to make that can use your values as the filter?
- Are there any friends or family you will share your values with? What about your colleagues or line manager?

A great way to share your values with others is to provide a PowerPoint deck or table that lists your values and then prompts others to share theirs with you. You can then proceed to a discussion of what you need from them and ask them what they need from you to enable you both to act according to your values.

EXERCISE: AUDITING YOUR LIFE AGAINST YOUR VALUES

Now you know your values, you can start to take an audit of your life to ensure that you are spending your time doing activities and projects that play to your values, with people who understand them. Doing this will allow you to live a fulfilled life. So, with that in mind, which activities, commitments, people and scenarios will you:

Stop being involved with?

Start being involved with?

Continue being involved with?

Be involved with more?

Be involved with less? (Don't be unrealistic here – there are many things you won't be able to cut out of your life entirely, but you can acknowledge that you want to do less of them to reduce their negative impact.)

Do what you love, and you will more than succeed, you will soar.
(Oprah Winfrey)[9]

I always knew when something didn't or did feel right to me, but up until I figured out my values and purpose, I couldn't clearly articulate why.

Discovering my values and purpose has helped me to clarify what is important to me and therefore enable quicker and better-informed decisions.

I think anyone can benefit from being clearer on what is important to them. Establishing it early in your life will help you to be much more self-aware, and therefore emotionally intelligent, and this will guide you through life.

(Nadine Singler, Head of Marketing and Sustainability, Krispy Kreme)

USING YOUR VALUES
TO DEFINE THE
RIGHT ROLE FOR YOU

One of the many benefits of defining your values is that you can use them in your work to choose roles and organizations with which your values are aligned. You can then aim for a work style and level of remuneration that will allow you live the life you have designed as a whole. You may want to come back to this section at the end of the unit to use inputs from later chapters.

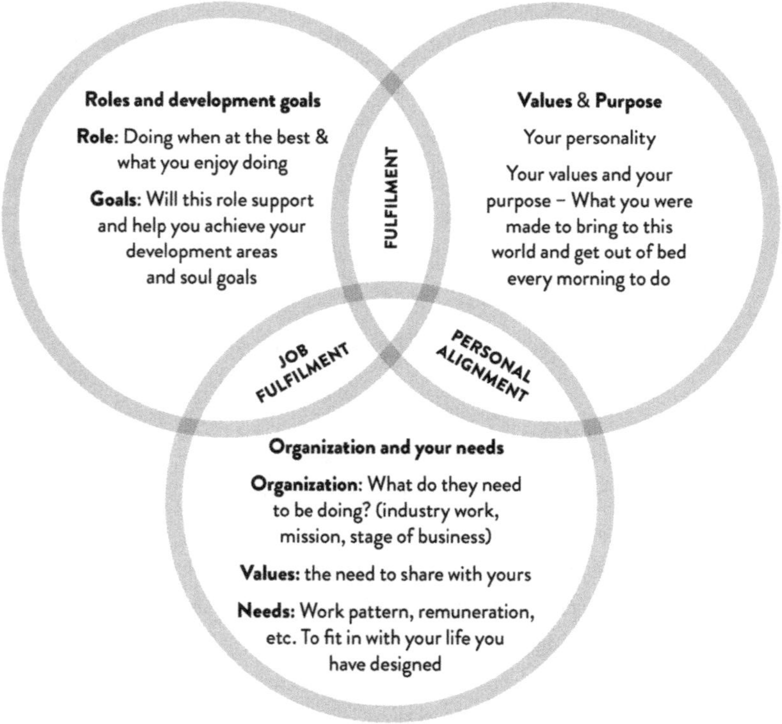

Roles and development goals

Role: Doing when at the best & what you enjoy doing

Goals: Will this role support and help you achieve your development areas and soul goals

FULFILMENT

Values & **Purpose**

Your personality

Your values and your purpose – What you were made to bring to this world and get out of bed every morning to do

JOB FULFILMENT

PERSONAL ALIGNMENT

Organization and your needs

Organization: What do they need to be doing? (industry work, mission, stage of business)

Values: the need to share with yours

Needs: Work pattern, remuneration, etc. To fit in with your life you have designed

FIGURE 13.1 INTERSECTION BETWEEN YOUR ROLE AND GOALS, YOUR VALUE AND PURPOSE, AND YOUR ORGANIZATION AND NEEDS

EXERCISE: DEFINING YOUR NEXT JOB

Role and goals

What type of task within your role would enable you to work in your zone of genius (what you are best at and what you enjoy)?

Would this role provide development opportunities? Would you be able to develop areas that would allow you to progress in your dream role and achieve your 'soul goals' (see *Chapter 14*)?

Which of your values would this role play to?

Values and purpose

Would the organization's values align with any of your personal values? If so, how?

Would the organization's purpose resonate with you and motivate you? Would it be aligned with your purpose? Would it allow you to live yours?

What industry motivates and interests you?

Lifestyle needs

What remuneration would you need to make the life you have defined happen?

What would you need to ensure work fits in with your life and not the other way around? (For example, flexible hours or a reduced work week to enable you to work on a side hustle.)

Having defined your ideal job, you don't necessarily need to find a new employer. Drafting a job role that serves the above needs and presenting it to your existing employer can be a proactive first step.

> I had a really clear list of three attributes that I'd sketched out when I left Graze of the kind of attributes that I wanted in the company I wanted to join.
>
> Firstly, the category had to be in health and wellbeing, which I just love, and it had to be cutting edge and fast growth. Secondly, I wanted part of it to be founder led and of course I wanted to respect the individual and the team and really importantly see my skill set fitting in. And then thirdly, size – I wanted to be in a start-up. I love the start-up world. There are highs and lows. And it also had to have a proven concept and probably have gone through seed funding ...
>
> My career highs have been when circumstances aligned with my values and they've involved two elements. One is obviously the synergistic effects of seeing what a bunch of people can do with a shared purpose when they are all driven toward the same goal. But also doing something really valuable for others with the power of the commercial entity.
>
> **(Emma Heal, Managing Director and Partner, Lucky Saint)**[10]

I was recently talking with Alex Hirst, co-founder and CEO of Hoxby Collective. We quickly identified that we could talk all day about the importance of bringing your whole self to work, and thinking about work and the role that it plays in your life as one of many elements of your goals and dreams.

Sometimes our best work doesn't happen between the hours of 9 to 5 (I'm sure you're probably thinking when the last time you worked 9 to 5 as a marketer was). The way in which we work is changing, with an increase in flexible working requests, thanks to Anna Whitehouse and the work of Flex Appeal[11] providing broader access and more tools to enable remote working.

There is a growing dislike for traditional working, with 60% of people unhappy in their jobs.[12] A desire to work with a more diverse group of people and an opportunity to advance our collective intelligence is leading to a new model of work emerging, which is more suited to the digital age we live in than the industrial one we have left behind.

Hoxby is pioneering a model of work that lets you decide for yourself when and where you work – your workstyle can fit work around your life, rather than life having to fit around work. Hirst has also strived to create a workforce, or bank of freelancers, that companies and brands can utilize to provide added resources and skills to their teams on a project-by-project basis. This big dream is a reality for Hoxby's 1,000+ members around the world.

> It's a shame to say this but putting your life before your work is an alien concept. It takes a lot of brainpower to make this switch away from being told when and where to work into deciding for yourself. It feels like we're taking liberties which, when you think about it, is absurd. That's why we are developing tools to help everyone with that transition because the benefits for those that do, on their mental health, physical health, wellbeing and productivity, are transformative.
>
> **(Alex Hirst, Co-founder and CEO of Hoxby Collective)[13]**

SKILLS AND TALENTS

Shortly we will look at defining your purpose – your 'why.' A key component of this is leveraging your skills and talents. A talent is a natural aptitude, whereas a skill is an ability to do things well.

What skills and talents do you possess that are natural gifts or that you have learned or developed? Consider:

- What are you naturally good at?
- What are you naturally skilled at?
- What skills have you learned?

YOUR PURPOSE OR 'WHY'

What is your purpose?

For me, purpose is the 'why' we get out of bed every morning. It goes beyond the surface level and is more than just making money and paying the bills. It's what we bring to the world – perhaps even why we were put on this earth.

One way of conceptualizing purpose is as follows:

Purpose = Values + Passions + Skills + Talents

Knowing your purpose as well as your values can help to guide you through life decisions and see where best to focus your time and energy. It might also give you a sense of direction and fulfilment in what you are doing.

FINDING YOUR WHY

There is a great book written by Simon Sinek, David Mead and Peter Docker called *Find Your Why*.[14] The authors state that the 'why' is the purpose, cause or belief that drives every one of us. They want to start a movement to inspire people to do the things that inspire them, and they offer a process to help you find clarity, meaning and fulfilment.

He who has a why to live for can bear almost any how.

(Friedrich Nietzsche)[15]

Find Your Why suggests the following method to define your why:

1. **Gather stories**: from your birth to date, collate the stories that hold significance or stand out to you
2. **Identify themes**: find a trusted partner to do this with, to share your stories while they cluster themes for you
3. **Draft your 'why'**: using the following structure:
   To ... (the contribution you make to others' lives)
   So that ... (the impact of your contribution)

SHARE TIME

My personal 'why' is:

To connect with businesses and people, providing knowledge, perspective and drive

So that they are empowered to make change and grow

The following exercise may help you think about your purpose or 'why.'

EXERCISE: WHY DO YOU GET OUT OF BED?

Why do you get out of bed every morning?

What were you born to do?

What do you want to be known for?

What can you be relied upon for?

What legacy do you want to leave behind?

Is this what you want to be doing?

What do you want to be doing instead?

How will this fulfil you?

What are your talents?

What skills or expertise do you have?

What are you passionate about?

Peter Docker explains that it's important to be mindful of where your purpose comes from:

It's like a bus driving along the road and on that bus there are two sets of seats either side the aisle. On one side of the aisle is fear and on the other side of the aisle there's love. On the fear side of the aisle there'll be drivers such as self-preservation at the expense of others, self-image or an urge to hide how we truly feel. Whereas on the love side of the bus there's things like standing for something bigger than ourselves, willingness to be vulnerable and let others into how we truly feel or an ability to see abundance where others may see scarcity. At any one particular time, those drivers – from either the love side of the bus or the fear side of the bus – are trying to grab hold of the driving wheel and steer us in a particular direction.

So, when we talk about things like purpose, for me we need to get really clear. Which side of the bus is driving us – is it things around love or is it things around fear? And of course, if we want to create something that's generative in the world, then it's most sustainable to choose something that comes from the love side of the bus.

(Peter Docker, Co-founder, Why Not Un Limited)[16]

CAPTURE TIME: KEY DISCOVERIES

1.

2.

3.

WHAT THREE THINGS ARE YOU GOING TO DO NEXT?

1.

2.

3.

CHAPTER SUMMARY

In this chapter, we looked at defining what drives and motivates you (your values) and what gets you out of bed every morning (your purpose and why). As a next step, I encourage you to think about how you are going to use this new found insight so you can truly embody your values in your day-to-day life. In the next chapter, we will look to define what it is you want from your life as a whole and to define your 'soul goals.'

CHAPTER 14

WHAT DO YOU WANT AND WHERE DO YOU WANT TO BE?

In this chapter we will look at what you want from life both professionally and personally. We will take the time to gain clarity on what you want, your goals, and your dreams and aspirations for your life today and in the future.

If you don't like the road you're walking, start paving another one.

(widely attributed to Dolly Parton)

LIFE BY DESIGN AND MAKING SPACE

I believe in the idea of life by design – life is not happening *to* us but happening *for* us. 'Life by design' is a term I use to describe the process of taking time to think about what we want out of life and the goals we want to achieve (as a whole, professionally and personally). This means getting clear visually on what that looks like, as if we were graphic designers putting together a mood board for our own life. What is it you want to be doing, feel like and have in your life by your own choosing?

As you take the time to design the life you want to have, it's not a case of 'out with the old and in with the new.' Instead, it's more about focusing on what you already have, what you don't want any more and what you want in the future. In *Chapter 13*, I encouraged you to define your values and use them as a filter to consider what existing activities you want to continue, stop doing or start doing so as to feel more fulfilled. You might even decide that you'd like to put those plans into action and live them for a while, before you start dreaming big with new goals. If so, that's fine – do that first and return to this chapter later.

The definition of insanity is doing the same thing over and over again but expecting different results.

(widely attributed to Albert Einstein)

You can do anything but not everything. So, ensure that you spend your time on activities that allow you to achieve your goals and live the life that you want to be living. We are in control of our destination. We design what we want our lives to look like by focusing on this forward-looking vision, making small movements every day toward achieving it.

TIME AND HEADSPACE

Just as you needed time and headspace to think about your personality (*Chapter 12*) and values (*Chapter 13*), you will need to make time and headspace to think about your goals in life.

SHARE TIME

An old colleague of mine once made time to meet me for lunch. She told me she felt aggrieved that she hadn't been recognized for what she had delivered for her organization during the years she had worked there, and was about to ask the owner when she would be eligible to become a share partner in the company.

My response was to ask, "Is that what you truly want?"

She thought for a moment, so I said, "Putting the share partner opportunity to one side, where do you want to be working in three years' time? Do you perhaps want to use your expertise to start your own business?"

"Yes," she replied. "That's my long-term plan."

I am telling you this story because it is a good example of how setting aside time (alone or with others) to assess our current situation can pay off. By simply taking the time out to meet up with someone else for an external view, my ex-colleague gained the headspace to realize that the battle she was about to face might not be the right one for her. It would be the obvious and expected next step on paper, but it wasn't what she truly wanted.

The advice I gave to this ex-colleague was to think about where she wanted to be in the next three years and consider what she needed to be doing to allow her to achieve the goal of having her own business. We worked out that what she actually needed was more time in her current organization, but not necessarily as a partner, so she could focus on learning wider practical skills (such as financial accounting) and close her knowledge gaps. We also took the time to look at what she was already able to do (her strengths and what she was known and relied upon for) that she could carry over into her future business. This included her ability to:

- Create visions for her clients
- Deliver award-winning campaigns by finding the most realistic way to bring these to life
- Create processes
- Listen well
- Maintain strong client relationships

We also thought about:

- What would her business offer?
- How would her business solve a customer problem differently from her future competitors?
- What partnerships and connections would she need to start building?
- What else would she need to do to bring her vision to life?

As a result, my ex-colleague felt confident she was moving in a new direction that would fulfil a personal and professional life goal.

QUESTIONS TO ASK YOURSELF

- Are you giving yourself headspace and time away from daily life to think about your goals?
- Do you prefer to think things through on your own or with someone else?
- Have you tried going for a walk to think things through?
- Would it benefit you to define your goals with the help of a coach?
- Have you tried talking out loud to a friend who will truly listen?

If you don't take the time to think big and get clarity, you'll never achieve what your heart truly desires. If you're struggling to get started, consider things that you have always wanted to do.

SETTING LIFE GOALS AND FINDING CLARITY

What is it that you truly desire? Not what you can practically do now but what you truly want? I am going to ask you to dream big and without restraints – no if, ands or buts.

As I've touched upon in earlier chapters, the key benefit of setting goals is fulfilment. Fulfilment comes from achieving something you desire. In order to feel fulfilled, you need to have clear goals – or at least clarity on what you want.

Therefore, clarity is the start of fulfilment. The two concepts go hand in hand. You are unlikely to feel fulfilled unless you are clear on what you want and what your goals are, and start making progress toward achieving those goals.

I believe fulfilment comes from doing something every day that embodies and plays to our values. It means ensuring that we take a step every day that brings us closer to our goals.

SOUL GOALS

I use the term 'soul goals' for goals that are truly connected to the core of your being. These are goals that you can see and feel with your deepest and most powerful emotions – or perhaps physically in the area of your solar plexus, which is midway up the centre of your chest, near your sternum. This is because the solar plexus is where your image and identity are said to lie within your body. This is quite a spiritual way of understanding life goals. If it doesn't resonate with you, that's fine.

We have one life, just one. Why aren't we running toward our wildest dreams like we are on fire?

(Anonymous)

EXERCISE: WHAT DO YOU TRULY WANT?

Let yourself dream big, without limitations. For now, put to one side practical considerations (the 'how'), realism and any negative thoughts about being able to achieve your goals. Also keep in mind that these goals are just for you – try not to include others' goals for you or your goals for others (e.g. your spouse or child). These are your goals and yours alone.

Think about the following questions:

- What do you want your life to look like now and in five years?

- What do you want to achieve in the next five years (or whatever time frame makes most sense to you)?

- What are your goals, both professionally and personally, for your life as a whole? (work, pastimes, experiences, relationships, etc.)

- How do you want to feel in five years' time? What will it take for you to feel like that?

- Is there something that you have always wanted to do?

- Is there something you used to do as a child and want to do again? Or make more time for?

- What don't you want to be happening in five years' time? (What you want will usually be the opposite of this.)

- What is your soul saying to you?

Sense-checking your goals

Once you have drafted a list of goals, consider the following points to ensure they are right for you:

- How do you feel when you think about what it will be like to achieve these goals?
- What will be the benefits to you of achieving these goals?
- How motivated are you to get started?
- How motivated are you to follow through on the steps required to achieve these goals?

Your goals

Capture your final list of goals here:

1.
2.
3.
4.
5.

Add more if you want (five is not the limit!).

CERTAINTY AND UNCERTAINTY

Another thing we need to feel fulfilled is the right mix of certainty and uncertainty. When we have certainty, we know what is going to happen and can devise a plan to follow. We have stability and a routine of activities that happen every day. This allows us to feel like we are rooted, grounded and secure.

In contrast, uncertainty encompasses all the unplanned events in life and requires us to learn how to adapt. New and unexpected things happen. This allows us to have variety in life.

As humans we are ideally looking for a combination of the two. Too much certainty and life becomes boring, but too much uncertainty and the wheels will start to come off. The clichéd idea of a midlife crisis usually comes about when someone has achieved everything in their life that they were previously striving for. Everything feels stable to the point of boredom – work, their daily routine, their home life and so on – and so they go off in search of variety, adventure or uncertainty.

This need for balance will affect how well your peers and colleagues (and your friends and family) will react to changes around them. This is something to be mindful of when you need to implement change within your business or team. If a member of your team has uncertainty happening outside work – perhaps an illness, a family argument or strained relationships – they may seek certainty within work and will find change harder to accept.

> *If we get total certainty, we get ... bored out of our minds. So, God, in Her infinite wisdom, gave us a second human need, which is uncertainty. We need variety. We need surprise.*
>
> **(Tony Robbins)**[17]

When looking at your goals, check whether they make you feel a mix of certainty (stability, security, etc.) and uncertainty (variety or something new) to ensure you have a fulfilling balance.

USING VISION BOARDS
TO BRING GOALS TO LIFE

Once you have defined your goals and dreams, it's time to bring them to life. A great way to do this is by creating a vision board to visually represent what your new life would look and feel like. There are a lot of different views behind how a vision board should work. They rose in popularity following the release of Rhonda Byrne's *The Secret*, which focuses on the 'law of attraction' and suggests that by visualizing what you want, you are emitting a powerful frequency out into the universe.[18]

HOW IT WORKS:
THE RETICULAR ACTIVATING SYSTEM

As a marketer, I tend to focus more on the science behind the idea of vision boards. The reticular activating system (RAS) is a part of the brain: a collection of nerves in the back of your head, in the brainstem. It filters what you see and hear to ensure that you focus on what is important to you or what you need. Our minds see something like 40,000 messages and images every day, so the RAS does a lot of filtering work.

The RAS has been there since humans evolved. In prehistoric times, it would focus on what we needed – for example, if we were hungry and needed food, the RAS would filter out the environment around us and focus on what would satisfy this need, whether that was a buffalo or berries.

Now, in modern times, the RAS focuses on other things that we tell ourselves we need. Have you ever noticed that when you are considering buying a new car, all you can see on the road are the models you're considering buying? Some readers may realize this is similar to the heightened awareness phase of buying behaviour that customers experience as part of their information search.

The RAS also looks for or focuses on things we see or hear that play to the narratives or beliefs in our minds. For example, one of my limiting beliefs is that I'm not very creative. As a consequence, whenever anybody around me says anything that could plausibly be interpreted as critiquing my creativity, my brain has a tendency to home in on it and disregard whatever else the person is saying. (There is more information on limiting beliefs in *Chapter 15*.)

The RAS is a powerful tool, and once we are clear on what we want in life, we can use it to our benefit. One way to use the RAS is to create a vision board. These not only allow us to clearly see what our goals are and what they look like but also ensure the RAS starts focusing on these goals, allowing us to notice and bring into focus anything that might relate to them. We can strengthen the connections between our goals by visualizing them. This also helps us to build an emotional connection with our goals by starting to feel what it will be like when we have achieved them.

To get what you really want in life, you need a clear goal that has purpose and meaning behind it. Once this is in place, you can focus your energy on the goal and become obsessive about it. When you learn how to focus your energy, amazing things happen.

(Tony Robbins)[19]

CREATING A VISION BOARD

Having defined your values and dreamed big across all aspects of your life, a vision board will enable you to visually reflect what you want your future life to look like and what goals you want to achieve. These could relate to:

- Relationships
- Home
- Work role
- Business direction

- Creative expression and interests
- Travel and adventure
- Health
- Spirituality
- Anything else that you want to achieve

To create your vision board, you will need the following:
- Thick card, foam board or a cork pinboard
- Scissors and glue, tape or pins
- Magazines or other sources of images (I recommend using Google Images) – use your answers to the exercises in *Chapter 13* and earlier in this chapter as inspiration when choosing images
- Paper to write or print on

Figure 14.1 shows one of my vision boards. If you came to my office, you would see it proudly displayed on top of my bookshelf. This ensures that I see it every day and remain focused. Additionally, others who see the board may ask me about it, which pushes me to explain and thereby get another accountability buddy or perhaps further clarity on what I am working toward and what I want from life.

FIGURE 14.1 MY VISION BOARD

You will see that the board covers all aspects of my life that are important to me: pastimes, work, family and me. I want you to think about work and life not as two separate things but as components of your total life – your whole self. One might fuel the other or they might be more separate – it's up to you what you want your life to look like.

Figure 14.2 shows another example, this time created by somebody I once coached. This moved me to tears when I saw it. Having helped her to define her values and set goals (which played to her values so she would feel fulfilled), I asked her to bring it all to life with a vision board. Forty-eight hours later, she sent me this. Why did it bring me to tears? Well, it brought to life exactly how she had verbally described her goals (probably the clearest I've encountered) and the life she wanted to create and live. She also added her values to her board to ensure that they would stay at the forefront of her mind and that she would achieve her goals while remaining true to her values.

FIGURE 14.2 A VISION BOARD CREATED BY SOMEBODY I HAVE COACHED

HOW COULD YOU USE VISION BOARDS WITH YOUR TEAM?

One option could be to run a values workshop with your team, provide some coaching to help them define their values and goals, and then ask them to create their own vision boards. You could then allow them to share their boards with the wider team to create a deeper sense of connection and encourage understanding of each other as individuals.

Alternatively, you might create a vision board together so that you can create a vision for the team that you are all part of.

Or you could just use vision boards practically as a way of bringing to life some of your customer personas. This could provide visual clarity on who your customers are, what they spend their time doing, and their beliefs, values and wants, to allow you to focus on their needs. Doing this could better enable you to get into the hearts and minds of your customers and keep them front of mind over the long term and in your daily decision-making. (See *Chapter 7* for more on this topic.)

CAPTURE TIME: KEY DISCOVERIES

1.

2.

3.

WHAT THREE THINGS ARE YOU GOING TO DO NEXT?

1.

2.

3.

CHAPTER SUMMARY

I hope that this chapter has enabled you to find clarity on what your goals are, how they will bring you fulfilment and how you can create a visual representation of what you are striving to achieve, thereby using the RAS to its full ability.

You are probably feeling a whole host of emotions – perhaps supercharged and excited to bring these goals and plans for yourself to life, alongside negative thoughts on how on earth you will make all of this happen in reality. The final two chapters of this book will explore ways of dealing with these varying emotions. In *Chapter 15* we will look at beliefs we hold about ourselves so you can deal with any negative thoughts and limiting beliefs that arise as you start to work toward your goals. And in *Chapter 16* we will explore some principles that you can follow to help you have the energy and drive to bring these plans to life. Fear not – I've got you ...

WHAT CAN PREVENT YOU FROM TAKING ACTION AND EMPLOYING THE MINDSET NEEDED TO ACHIEVE AND GROW?

In *Chapter 14* we looked at what you want, your goals and the importance of bringing them to life. I'm sure, as you were writing these goals or creating your vision board, negative thoughts or beliefs may have been coming up in your head. In order to move forward, we need to work through these. This chapter aims to explain beliefs we hold about ourselves, help you identify and address limiting beliefs, and allow you to understand the importance of having a growth mindset to keep moving forward every day beyond your comfort zone and toward your goals.

WHAT ARE LIMITING BELIEFS?

Limiting beliefs are beliefs we form that have a negative impact. They are statements that we say out loud or in our head that stop us from being able to achieve our goals – excuses, if you like. Usually a limiting belief is a false belief that you hang onto and that gets in the way of you taking action toward achieving a goal. It is something you say or believe – a bit like a voice in your head that constrains you in some way.

Beliefs can also be positive. They may even underpin some of the self-confidence you have in certain areas of your life.

I have gained a great deal of insight from taking the time to understand my own limiting beliefs. I also now can't help but notice them coming from all the people who surround me – my friends, family, colleagues, clients and so on. Here are some of the most common I hear:

- 'I can't start my own business because I'm not good with numbers'
- 'I'm not as clever as so-and-so'
- 'I would never have the confidence to do that'

- 'I haven't got the time'
- 'I would never make any money doing that'
- 'I'm not good at public speaking or putting myself out there'

I could go on ...

EXERCISE: QUICK BELIEF CHECK

What beliefs do you have that are stopping you from pursuing your goals?

What would you have achieved, if you weren't carrying this belief?

What beliefs are *helping* you to pursue your goals?

HOW ARE BELIEFS FORMED?

Both positive and negative beliefs are usually formed as a result of the influence of a person of authority, an emotion and our susceptibility. The process is shown in *Figure 15.1.*

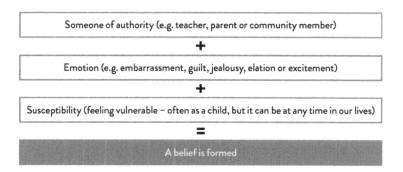

FIGURE 15.1 HOW BELIEFS ARE FORMED

Beliefs are usually formed before we reach the age of eight, due to our having a higher level of susceptibility at this age. But they can be formed at any time throughout our lives when we are feeling susceptible – for example, during a life change such as a new job.

SHARE TIME

As I mentioned in the previous chapter, one of my limiting beliefs is that I'm not very creative. Having identified this, I took the time to work out where it came from and who prompted it. I realized that it had come from a teacher (person of authority), when I was feeling embarrassed (emotion), while I was at school (susceptibility). Since that time I have carried this belief with me.

But we are all works in progress and we can address our limiting beliefs (as I will explain shortly).

I am going to ask you to take the time to be honest and reflective with yourself to identify your limiting beliefs. The first step of overcoming them is identifying them. Once you have identified and acknowledged them, you can work on and through them.

EXERCISE: IDENTIFYING YOUR LIMITING BELIEFS

You can do this exercise either with or without the goals in front of you that you defined in *Chapter 14*.

Your limiting beliefs
What limiting beliefs do you have?

Who says them to you? Or whose voice do you hear when they are manifested in your head?

Concentrate on one of the beliefs (you can repeat these questions for each belief if you wish). Where did this belief come from?

Can you remember the situation where it arose?

Can you review it logically and break it down as I did above?

Acknowledging your limiting beliefs
Having identified your limiting beliefs, let's take the first step by acknowledging them and how they are currently serving you. Again, pick one belief to concentrate on, but you can repeat the questions

for other beliefs.

Has the belief stopped you from achieving something in the past?

What opportunities have you already passed up by hanging on to your limiting belief?

What negative situations have you experienced as a result of hanging on to your limiting belief?

What would you really like to do if you could overcome this belief?

Letting go of your limiting beliefs
Does your belief hold any value?

Do you want to keep this belief?

Are you ready to start addressing it?

If you are ready, then let's look to reframe or disregard each belief using either or both of the tools below.

ADDRESSING LIMITING BELIEFS

The two main ways you can address limiting beliefs are to disregard them or to reframe them.

DISREGARDING

Disregarding a belief means stopping it recurring in your internal or external narrative, or at least training yourself to react to it differently when it arises – for example, by saying, "I have dealt with that, thanks" or "Here are all the reasons why it's not true."

To do this, think about all the evidence you have that proves your belief isn't accurate in reality. Think about your assumptions and break them down.

For example, in response to my limiting belief that I'm not very creative, I might remind myself that I am creative as I have developed many new marketing models and processes, and I use my creativity to solve problems. This rewrites the narrative in your brain.

REFRAMING

Reframing gives you a new narrative to tell yourself or an affirmation you can use to change your belief. For example, one of your limiting beliefs might be that you are not good at writing. When this thought comes up, you could remind yourself that:

- Each day you write strategies, blogs and correspondence that are positively received
- You write to help people
- You can just write and then edit later

When you choose to use reframing, ensure that each time the thought or belief arises, you state the reframed statement to yourself clearly in your head or out loud. It will take time for the belief to fully disappear, but the new narrative will eventually embed and the old belief will become less of a barrier.

TOP TIPS FOR REFRAMING

If you are a visual person, write your new narrative on a piece of paper or sticky note and rip it up when you feel you have largely removed the limiting belief. Then write your next reframed statement and put it somewhere where you will see it daily.

EXERCISE: ADDRESSING YOUR LIMITING BELIEFS

Think about your limiting beliefs.
Which ones do you want to keep?

Which ones do you want to disregard?

Which ones do you want to reframe or rewrite?

WHAT DRIVES YOU?

Transactional analysis (TA) is a concept developed by the psychiatrist Eric Berne, who built a series of models around our personality and systems for personal growth.[20] We all have the ability to think, feel and behave as we desire, and we can make the decision to change ourselves and our destiny. However, in order to do this we need to look at our drivers and our ego states.

Berne also identified that we tend to receive our drivers from our parents or others in a position of authority when we are young, usually before the age of eight (are you seeing a theme here?). When we feel challenged or stressed, we usually begin to manifest behaviours linked to our drivers to help us deal with these feelings – in other words, we often revert to our child self.

Following are the five drivers Berne identified in his work on TA. Have a read through and see whether any resonate with you.

BE STRONG

This is common in men due to society's gender norms. According to the 'be strong' driver, when we are struggling we should hide our emotions, suck it up and get on with it. People with this driver are good in a crisis but they can find it difficult to act according to their feelings and can switch off when they experience personal or professional problems.

Internal voice: "Suck it up – don't let them see you are weak"
Physical signs: immobile face, stiff movement, rigid body

HURRY UP

People with the 'hurry up' driver are always hurtling about and rarely relax. They tend to eat and speak quickly, and they may struggle to live in the moment and enjoy what they are doing. Some people with this driver are very productive but many frequently feel tired and unfulfilled.

Internal voice: "Get to the point," "You will never get it done on time"
Physical signs: restless body (fidgeting, tapping), speaking quickly, impatient expression, not paying attention

TRY HARD

People with the 'try hard' driver are up for anything but often drop off before the end (they get bored and give up) or feel that their endeavour is always incomplete. They tend to get frustrated and may have a recurring sense of failure.

Internal voice: "You've got to try harder"
Physical signs: tense stomach or shoulders, leaning in

BE PERFECT

People with the 'be perfect' driver want everything to be just right. They are willing to go to great lengths to ensure details are 'just so' and want things to be exactly right. As a result, they may produce high-quality work, but potentially at the price of excessive amounts of time and anxiety.

Internal voice: "This isn't good enough," "You could do better"
Physical signs: precise and clipped speech, rigid and upright posture

PLEASE OTHERS

People with the 'please others' driver want to ensure everyone is happy, but this is often to their own detriment. They have a tendency to associate with people who are less likely to want to please them in return, which can ultimately lead to resentment. They often have a large circle of friends and take good care of their family, but they may neglect their own needs.

Internal voice: "You have to say 'yes' or they won't like you"
Physical signs: leaning forward, nodding, smiling

SHARE TIME

I am a combination of 'please others' and 'hurry up.' What driver do you think you are? Or are you a combination?

FIND OUT YOUR DRIVERS

Following is a link to a questionnaire that can help you to define your drivers. It lists positive and negative attributes of each and gives some tips on how to interact with others who possess certain key drivers.

https://www.psychosynthesiscoaching.co.uk/wp-content/uploads/2017/11/StressDriversQuestionnairePGPCL2015.pdf

---

MINDSET

Mindset is what separates the best from the rest.

(Jo Owen)[21]

Having a positive mindset and belief that you can achieve is key. This takes time, especially if you are currently not in a positive mental space and have habitually told yourself many limiting beliefs. You are going to have to get into the right mindset to make change or find the energy to grow.

Mindset can be considered to have two types:

- **Fixed mindset** people believe their qualities, skills, ability and situation are fixed. They often think that anything good that comes their way will be luck. Example thoughts: "I can't do that," "I only know how to do this."
- **Growth mindset** people believe that their qualities, skills, abilities and situation can all be developed and grow. Through hard work, their situation can change and improve. Example thoughts: "I can't do that yet," "I need to learn x if I want to achieve y."

	FIXED	GROWTH
SKILLS	You are born with a finite set of skills	You can always learn new skills
CHALLENGES	Oppose	Embrace
	Avoid trying to overcome or give up easily	Use as opportunities to learn
EFFORT	Don't see the point as "What will be will be"	See effort as essential to achieving goals: "Life's what you make it"
FEEDBACK	Defensive	Use as something to learn from
	List excuses as to why not to take on board	Use as action plans to work toward
SETBACKS	Pass the blame onto others	Use as a sign of the need to work harder or differently
	Complain about the situation but less likely to take action or keep going	

TABLE 15.1 FIXED AND GROWTH MINDSETS

People with a growth mindset still feel disappointment and anger, but they tend to move through the grief curve more quickly and have a greater level of resilience (see *Chapter 9*). They are quicker to bounce back, seeing the positives and having a drive to improve. Whereas endurance (linked with a fixed mindset) means that you will keep going, having resilience (linked with a growth mindset) means you will think about what you can do to improve your situation.

Having a fixed mindset will more than likely limit you or the speed with which you can achieve your goals. Having a growth mindset is preferable as it means you are more likely to grow and develop to achieve your goals.

MOVING OUT OF
YOUR COMFORT ZONE

In order to grow, you will need to move out of your comfort zone. When you are in your comfort zone, you are not growing and are doing only things you know how to do, day in and day out.

If you are happy in your comfort zone, then that's great. However, I'm assuming you are reading this chapter because you have a goal you want to achieve – or perhaps you want to help someone to achieve theirs personally or professionally. In order for you (or them) to grow, you (or they) will need to move through the phases outlined below.

The key phase is fear. You need to acknowledge the fear and work through it to learn a new skill, or achieve the growth or goals that you desire. It is normal to experience a feeling of fear when we do something new for the first time. Your brain sends you feelings of fear to warn you that you are doing something dangerous or new and to be more alert. Thank your brain for the warning, acknowledge it and keep going.

The phases are:

- **Comfort zone (unconscious competence)**: you are performing skills with ease, maybe even automatically – you feel safe and in control as this is the easiest place to be, but you are not growing
- **Fear zone (conscious incompetence)**: you are aware that you don't understand what you need to know or do – you lack self-confidence to start and are procrastinating
- **Learning zone (conscious competence)**: you are aware that you are acquiring new skills but not yet proficient – you are dealing with overcoming new challenges or learning new skills
- **Growth zone (unconscious competence)**: you are feeling proficient in skills and fulfilled that you have achieved

your goal, and are hopefully celebrating this (see *Chapter 16*) – you are living according to your purpose and values, and maybe even thinking about what you might want to achieve next

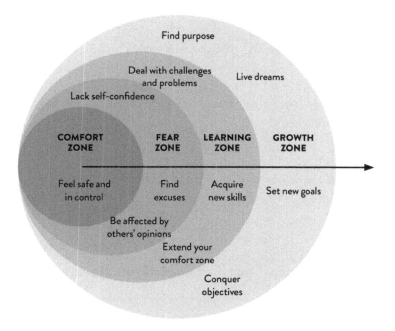

FIGURE 15.2 THE FOUR ZONES

If you are struggling to move through the fear stage, the following exercise may help.

EXERCISE: PROOF POINTS

Start by celebrating what you have achieved so far: what you have now is what you once longed for.

What did you once want and have now?

What have you achieved in the past year alone?

What has been your greatest achievement to date (by your measure only – no one else's)?

What can you do now that you once found hard?

Take the first step – even if it's small. Go on, I believe in you!

CAPTURE TIME: KEY DISCOVERIES

1.

2.

3.

WHAT THREE THINGS ARE YOU GOING TO DO NEXT?

1.

2.

3.

CHAPTER SUMMARY

In this chapter, we looked at identifying the negative beliefs that have held you back in the past or are currently holding you back. This process may be quite uncomfortable, especially as you break these beliefs down and look at ways to disregard or reframe them. Adopting a positive mindset while you move through your comfort zone and past the fear zone is essential.

New negative or limiting beliefs may arise at a later stage, but don't let this stop you. Come back to this chapter, break down how each belief was formed, and look to disregard or reframe it. Stick with the process – the discomfort will pass as your brain takes on board the new belief. It will all be worth it when you achieve your goals.

In the next chapter, we will explore some tools, techniques and principles you can use to keep yourself on track to achieving your goals, day by day.

CHAPTER 16

PRINCIPLES TO USE TO BRING YOUR PLANS AND GOALS TO LIFE

Throughout this unit, you have taken the time to define your values and goals, gain clarity on what these would look like in your life, and started to address any limiting beliefs that may be holding you back. In this final chapter of the book, we will look at some concepts, principles and techniques that will support you and ensure you maintain your energy, motivation and focus so you can achieve your goals. Marketing is a great career but also a highly pressured one, so in this chapter you will find thoughts on how to achieve your goals but also on how to tackle and manage daily challenges.

You may choose to use some or all of the ideas in this chapter. Do whatever works for you – as well as whatever is already working for you – to ensure you reach your goals, as that's where fulfilment lies.

You may be starting to feel overwhelmed about where you will find the time to pursue your goals on top of your work, family and personal commitments – especially if some of your 'soul goals' (see *Chapter 14*) aren't work or family related. The key is to break them down into bite-sized tasks, little by little. You will get there – I promise you. You don't have to do everything all at once and, in fact, please don't, as this will overwhelm you and possibly stop you from doing anything else. Finally, you certainly don't have to do it all alone. It is more than okay to ask for help from those who have gone before you.

MAKING IT HAPPEN

The remainder of this chapter offers suggestions on how to make your plans and goals a reality.

SETTING TIME-DEFINED TASKS

Not dissimilar to the process of setting your brand or business's vision and long-term goals (see *Chapters 2–4*), it can help to break your personal goals down into tasks to be completed over certain time frames (such as annually or every week). Look at each of your goals and start to think about what the key milestones will be to make them happen. Try to make them SMART if you can (see *Chapter 3*).

Personally, I set annual goals based on my vision board (see *Chapter 14*). I then set myself three tasks for each month, planning one month ahead, and break those down into three tasks for each week.

You can break your goals down into tasks within any time frame that you feel is manageable.

2 MM CHANGES AND TAKING IMMEDIATE ACTION

Take time every day to focus on your goals, whether that's looking at your vision board, meditating, or making small progress steps. Tony Robbins calls these 2 mm changes.[22]

Another approach is proposed by Mel Robbins, author of *The 5 Second Rule*.[23] She says that if you get an idea on how to make progress, take action immediately. If you don't, fear will kick in and stop you from doing it. Count backwards from five and just do it. For example, if you get the idea that you should call so-and-so, count "five, four, three, two, one" and pick up the phone (leave a message if they're not there).

Part of the reason this can work is that our brain associates countdowns with significant moments and opportunities to achieve, such as rocket blast offs and running a race.

SHARE TIME

One of my previous goals was to have a house in Cornwall. This was for several personal reasons. Firstly, I discovered that Cornwall, and Porth Beach in particular, is my happy place. Being there is the yin to my daily yang – it is my spiritual home, if you like. Secondly, while the house was important for my happiness and mental health, it also made sense once I became self-employed, and it was a wise invest-ment for my son's future and ultimately my own. I placed it on my vision board and spent some time every day visualizing what it would look, feel, be, taste and smell like to be there. I imagined it as if it were really happening, to ensure my reticular activating system was activated (see *Chapter 14*) and would focus on the goal.

Having gained clarity on this goal, I took steps every day toward making it happen. No matter how big or small, I would do something every day. These were some of my 2 mm moves:

- Call a friend for a mortgage broker recommendation
- Email a mortgage broker
- Ask how much I could borrow
- Understand how it works to buy a rental
- Work out how much I needed to save
- Set up a search on Rightmove in the area where I was looking to buy
- Build a plan to raise the remaining deposit funds
- Schedule a flight to Cornwall to view houses
- Line up viewings
- Speak to someone who had bought a holiday home to understand the pros and cons

I sit writing this section of the book in that said house and am about to take a break to walk to my 'soul beach,' having reached a 2 mm goal of writing 2,000 words today. Working toward your goals every day really does make them happen.

That said, I also want to share some realities. The above list of 2 mm changes might make it seem like the process was simple, but I had many challenges along the way, both practically and emotionally. Some new limiting beliefs came up that I needed to address. These kinds of difficulties are completely normal, especially when we are out of our comfort zone. Some of the struggles I experienced were as follows:

- Delay in completion date on the house
- Difficulty getting a mortgage for the house given its build type (eco house)

- Having to find a new mortgage
- Going over budget on the house's furnishings as I hadn't realistically set enough aside
- Panic that I wouldn't be able to rent it out, creating a financial risk for myself and my family

How did I overcome these obstacles? I talked things out with friends and in some cases professionals, but most importantly I spent time focusing on what it would feel like to be in the house – the benefits emotionally for me and my family and everyone else who got to stay there. I told everyone who would listen what I was doing, and this made me hold myself to account. Finally, I continued to visualize daily what the end benefit would look and feel like.

Keep going, because you didn't come this far to only come this far.

SCHEDULING TIME TO REFLECT ON YOUR PROGRESS

Just as you would have quarterly or monthly reviews for your brand strategy, I recommend you do the same for yourself. I often go away somewhere for the day or overnight on my own to take stock of where I am in working toward my goals. I think about whether there is anything that is jarring with my values or whether there are any values I have not been able to embody as often as I would like. Then I plan what I am going to do or how I will refocus to bring myself back into alignment, just as I would plan to ensure that I am delivering my brand goals for the year (e.g. by building a gap analysis or remedial action plan).

CELEBRATING SUCCESS

Celebrating your success is key for your brain to see a positive reward for the time and energy you have put in to working toward your goals. It doesn't have to be extravagant, but acknowledging and rewarding yourself for wins along the way will incentivize you and keep you motivated to keep going. It will also help you to build your confidence and acknowledge your progress and achievement.

CLEARING MENTAL SPACE

In order to focus on delivering both against your goals and in your role on a day-to-day basis, you need as much mental headspace as possible. Reflect on the following questions:

- Is there anything that is occupying your mind that you need to address?
- Are there any commitments you no longer want to continue with?
- Are you making time each day to just be, identifying anything that is filling your head that is not helpful and thinking about how to readdress and regroup?
- If you have recently experienced a worry (e.g. a conflict with a loved one or a colleague), have you had time to review this and why it bothered you?
- Have you captured the lessons you learned?
- Have you taken the time to gain perspective? A scale of awfulness can help here. On a scale of 1 to 10, where 10 is the most awful thing you can think of, where is your concern? Have you dealt with worse?

And this too shall pass.[24]

GROUNDING AND RECONNECTING
WITH YOURSELF DAILY

What's in your toolkit that you can use to ground yourself and improve your resilience levels? (See *Chapter 9* for more on resilience.) Following are some ideas for how to calm your sympathetic nervous system (which deals with our reactions to stress and danger):

- Morning or evening meditation

- Morning or evening visualizations
- Keeping a gratitude diary to capture three highlights from each day
- Journaling daily to capture thoughts, feelings and learnings
- Yoga to aid in the regulation of stress
- Taking a walk in nature – this is great for gaining perspective, and the rhythm of walking calms the mind and makes space for ideas to arise on how to solve a situation or goal
- Priming or breathing exercises that encourage you to make a shift in your thoughts and emotional state
- Time on your own daily to regroup and reflect

And do anything else that you know grounds you, such as chatting with a good friend or family member, exercising or listening to music. Make sure to support your team in doing what works for them too.

EXERCISE: CELEBRATE SUCCESS

Use this exercise to consider how you might implement the principles suggested in this chapter so far.

Which goals are you going to focus on?

Which tasks need to happen to allow those goals to come to life?

What are you going to do by the end of the year, month and week toward achieving these goals?

How will you log your progress?

How will you celebrate the success of achieving these milestones?

What daily ritual will you build to ensure you have time to ground your-self? Or prime yourself to take on the day with a positive mindset?

What do you have in your toolkit to help you gain perspective or over-come a challenge, so you can bounce back quickly with resilience?

SOCIAL MEDIA DETOX

It's time to detox your social media. You don't have to cull it altogether, although all credit to you if you can. But do ensure you are constantly adding and removing sources according to what reflects your goals – in this way, you can make your social media a kind of walking vision board. Use your social media to reflect the life you want to live, and follow people who have already achieved goals similar to yours (proof that it's possible).

Finally, ensure you remove anything that will drain any of your energy. There are two types of people in life: radia-tors and drainers. Remove and reduce your time spent with the drainers and spend more time with the radiators.

KEEPING YOUR PHYSICAL ENERGY UP

It's important to look after yourself to ensure you have the energy to make a change – specifically, by getting at least eight hours of sleep a day, ensuring you have the right food that will positively affect your energy levels, and being mindful of things that reduce your energy (e.g. drinking too much alcohol).

Physical exercise increases endorphins. Whatever the form of exercise you choose, if it can help you to increase your energy and in turn achieve your goals, then I'm sure you will agree it's worth it. You can also change your energy levels, especially during an afternoon slump, by doing simple activities such as stretching, dancing or even just listening to uplifting music.

GETTING OUTSIDE HELP

Who do you have around you to help and support you to achieve your goals? You don't have to do it all on your own.

You are caught up in the myth that you only have your own strength to rely on.

(Gabrielle Bernstein)[25]

Do you have the help you need from others to succeed? Following are some potential sources of help:
- **Accountability buddy**: a person who holds you to account for your actions and helps you maintain your motivation
- **Coach**: a person who helps you define what you want to achieve
- **Mentor**: a person who advises you on how to do things, as an expert in the field or topic you want to grow in
- **Teacher**: a person who imparts their knowledge to close a skill gap

You may need all four sources of help – don't be afraid to ask. Ultimately, look to find someone who has achieved what you want to achieve and ask for help or advice.

Knowledge isn't power; it's potential power. Execution trumps knowledge any day of the week.

(Tony Robbins)[26]

SHARE TIME

I've used both coaches and mentors – coaches on my journey to define my goals, vision and values, and mentors to help me in areas where I didn't have the skill set I needed. Two years into my business, I realized that I was going to have to proactively go and get new work, so I found a business development mentor. We met monthly and she advised on what I needed to do and held me to account for my actions. Over time, as I learned the new skills, I no longer needed this mentor, but we remain in regular contact. My current mentor is advising me on scaling up my consultancy, which is another skill I have not needed to use before, having been in client-side roles. Keep in mind that you can have more than one coach or mentor at the same time.

Also make sure that the friends and family members you surround yourself with will support your goals. You need people who will run alongside you, not hold you back; people who are as passionate and supportive about your goals as you are.

SHARING YOUR GOALS WITH OTHERS

Nothing makes a goal more real than saying it out loud and telling others what you are doing. One benefit of doing this is that you gain clarity on what you are doing each time you say your goal out loud to someone. It also helps to bring the goal to life, moving it from being an idea in a journal or in your head to something that you are actually doing. Finally, it helps with accountability as the more people you share your goal with, the more likely they are to check in and ask how you are getting on.

DREAM TEAM

As Jim Rohn says, "You are the average of the five people you spend the most time with."[27]

Jim Rohn talks about how important it is to surround yourself with positive influences when you are pursuing your dreams.[28] The people with whom you surround yourself with will greatly influence your success. They say five is the magic number. Have a think about who the five people are that you currently spend the most time with, or who will give you the most support and advice to help you achieve your dreams. If you are one-fifth of each of the people you surround yourself with, who do you want to make up your 100%? If this were a team you were building, who would you want in your dream team? I call this your party of five.

EXERCISE: GETTING YOUR DREAM TEAM IN PLACE

Who can you ask to be your accountability buddy?

Who are you running with? Do they support your goals and are they rooting for you?

Is there someone you would like to mentor or advise you, perhaps an expert in a skill you don't have but would like to learn?

Who do you want in your dream team of five people?

Do you need a coach to help give you the support, time and head-space to overcome any concerns or help you find clarity?

Who could you ask to teach you a skill?

CAPTURE TIME: KEY DISCOVERIES

1.

2.

3.

WHAT THREE THINGS ARE YOU GOING TO DO NEXT?

1.

2.

3.

CHAPTER SUMMARY

I hope this final chapter has filled you with the belief that you can achieve your goals and provided you with ideas, tools and techniques that will help you take action toward planning and achieving your goals and maintaining energy and motivation in your day-to-day marketing role. Applying the time and energy to develop you is just as important as developing your technical and soft skills as you bring your whole self to work and become the whole marketer for our ever-changing industry.

Thank you for taking the time to work on you.

CONCLUSION

I hope you feel it has been worth it to take the time out to work on yourself and your marketing career. As you read each of the three units, or dipped in and out, I'm sure you will have experienced a variety of thoughts, learnings and reflections. You may have had moments of confirmation on what you already know and are doing well in, moments where you refreshed your knowledge, moments where you identified and acknowledged where you could and should develop your skills further, and moments of learning or reflection.

You will have entered this book at a stage of your marketing career that is specific to you, with your own orientations within your business, your own particular role scope, and levels of competency that are unique to you. My hope is that you are concluding the book with clarity and a list of actions and learnings that you can take forward into development plans and daily practice, both to guide yourself and to help you guide those in your care.

Marketing's scope and landscape are ever-changing, as are the skills we need to develop on a day-to-day basis. Perhaps this book will provide you with a line-in-the-sand moment to enable you to assess where you are now and where you want to be moving forward, professionally and personally.

I also hope the book starts a ripple effect, encouraging leaders who are visionaries that inspire, lead and motivate – leaders who are human, authentic and honest and who think about those in their care as individuals, as 'wholes.' Each person is a whole marketer, with technical skills (what they do), soft skills (how they do it) and personal understanding (why they do it and what they need to feel fulfilled).

My ultimate goal is that you will end this book with a deeper understanding of yourself, what you want and need as a person, and the importance this plays in gaining fulfilment, personally and professionally.

I also hope this book has allowed you time to reflect; provided you with clarity, inspiration, guidance, support and empowerment; and most importantly, started your journey to a more successful and fulfilling career and life as a whole.

You are the person behind the brand and business. You hold the most important role in your organization – working within the function that drives the organization and its growth – so I ask you to stand in your power, and own your role and your career.

ENDNOTES

UNIT 1: TECHNICAL SKILLS

1. "Pete Markey CMO Boots UK" (*The Whole Marketer Podcast*, episode 20), accessed 1 January 2020, https://traffic.libsyn.com/secure/ thewholemarketer/Podcast_20_CMO_1.mp3.

2. "Conviction: Anthony Fletcher CEO Graze.com" (*The Whole Marketer Podcast*, episode 4), accessed 9 December 2020, https://traffic.libsyn. com/secure/thewholemarketer/podcast_4_Conviction.mp3.

3. "Leadership: Katherine Whitton, CMO Specsavers" (*The Whole Marketer Podcast*, episode 12), accessed 9 December 2020, https://thewholemarketer.libsyn.com/episode-12-leadership-with-guest-katherine-whitton.

4. "Competencies: Gemma Butler, Marketing Director, CIM" (*The Whole Marketer Podcast*, episode 8), accessed 9 December 2020, https://traffic.libsyn.com/secure/thewholemarketer/Podcast_8_ Compentencies_2.mp3.

5. "Pete Markey CMO Boots UK" (*The Whole Marketer Podcast*, episode 20), accessed 1 January 2020, https://traffic.libsyn.com/secure/ thewholemarketer/Podcast_20_CMO_1.mp3.

6. "Social Media: Michelle Carvill, Director, Carvill Creative" (*The Whole Marketer Podcast*, episode 6), accessed 9 December 2020, https://traffic. libsyn.com/secure/thewholemarketer/podcast_6_social_media.mp3.

7. "Leadership: Katherine Whitton, CMO Specsavers" (*The Whole Marketer Podcast*, episode 12), https://thewholemarketer.libsyn.com/episode-12-leadership-with-guest-katherine-whitton.

8. "Competencies: Gemma Butler, Marketing Director, CIM" (*The Whole Marketer Podcast*, episode 8), accessed 9 December 2020, https://traffic.libsyn.com/secure/thewholemarketer/Podcast_8_Compentencies_2.mp3.

9. "Conviction: Anthony Fletcher CEO Graze.com" (*The Whole Marketer Podcast*, episode 4), accessed 9 December 2020, https://traffic.libsyn.com/secure/thewholemarketer/podcast_4_Conviction.mp3.

10. Paul R. Smith, *SOSTAC®: Guide to Your Perfect Digital Marketing Plan* (n.p.: prsmith.org, 2020).

11. Paul R. Smith, *SOSTAC®: Guide to Your Perfect Digital Marketing Plan* (n.p.: prsmith.org, 2020).

12. "Commercial: Emma Heal" (*The Whole Marketer Podcast*, episode 3), accessed 9 December 2020, https://traffic.libsyn.com/secure/thewholemarketer/podcast_3_Commercial.mp3.

13. Ronnie Clifford, Instagram.

14. Simon Sinek, *Start with Why* (New York: Portfolio, 2009).

15. Simon Sinek, David Mead and Peter Docker, *Find Your Why* (London: Portfolio, 2017).

16. Simon Sinek, *Leaders Eat Last* (New York: Portfolio, 2014).

17. Simon Sinek, *The Infinite Game* (New York: Portfolio, 2019).

18. "Agile Marketing: Rachel Chapman" (*The Whole Marketer Podcast*, episode 15), accessed 9 December 2020, https://traffic.libsyn.com/secure/thewholemarketer/podcast_15_Agile.mp3.

19. "Agile Marketing: Rachel Chapman" (*The Whole Marketer Podcast*, episode 15), accessed 9 December 2020, https://traffic.libsyn.com/secure/thewholemarketer/podcast_15_Agile.mp3.

20. "Agile Marketing: Rachel Chapman" (*The Whole Marketer Podcast*, episode 15), accessed 9 December 2020, https://traffic.libsyn.com/secure/thewholemarketer/podcast_15_Agile.mp3.

21. "Agile Marketing: Rachel Chapman" (*The Whole Marketer Podcast*, episode 15), accessed 9 December 2020, https://traffic.libsyn.com/secure/thewholemarketer/podcast_15_Agile.mp3.

22. Alan G. Lafley and Roger L. Martin, *Playing to Win: How Strategy Really Works* (Boston: Harvard Business Review Press, 2013).

23. Alan G. Lafley and Roger L. Martin, *Playing to Win: How Strategy Really Works* (Boston: Harvard Business Review Press, 2013).

24. Byron Sharp, *How Brands Grow: What Marketers Don't Know* (Melbourne: Oxford University Press, 2010).

25. "Insight: Richard Bambrick" (*The Whole Marketer Podcast*, episode 11), accessed 9 December 2020, https://traffic.libsyn.com/secure/thewholemarketer/podcast_11_Insight__1.mp3.

26. Les Binet and Peter Field, *The Long and the Short of It* (London: Institute of Practitioners in Advertising, 2013).

27. "Digital: Daniel Rowles" (*The Whole Marketer Podcast*, episode 5), accessed 9 December 2020, https://traffic.libsyn.com/secure/thewholemarketer/podcast_5_Digital_2.mp3.

28. "Social Media: Michelle Carvill, Director, Carvill Creative" (*The Whole Marketer Podcast*, episode 6), accessed 9 December 2020, https://traffic.libsyn.com/secure/thewholemarketer/podcast_6_social_media.mp3.

29. "Digital: Daniel Rowles" (*The Whole Marketer Podcast*, episode 5), accessed 9 December 2020, https://traffic.libsyn.com/secure/thewholemarketer/podcast_5_Digital_2.mp3.

30. Dominique Turpin, "The CMO is Dead" (*Forbes*), last modified 3 October 2012, https://www.forbes.com/sites/onmarketing/2012/10/03/the-cmo-is-dead.

31. "Consumer Experience: Meredith O'Shaughnessy" (*The Whole Marketer Podcast*, episode 2), accessed 9 December 2020, https://traffic.libsyn.com/secure/thewholemarketer/podcast_2_Consumer_Behaviour.mp3.

32. "Global Leadership and Innovation: Shweta Harit" (*The Whole Marketer Podcast*), accessed 9 December 2020, https://traffic.libsyn.com/secure/thewholemarketer/Podcast_16_Leadership__Innovation_2.mp3.

33. "Digital: Daniel Rowles" (*The Whole Marketer Podcast*, episode 5), accessed 9 December 2020, https://traffic.libsyn.com/secure/ thewholemarketer/podcast_5_Digital_2.mp3.

34. Annmarie Hanlon, "The AIDA model" (Smart Insights), last accessed 24 March 2021, https://www.smartinsights.com/traffic-building-strategy/offer-and-message-development/aida-model/.

35. "Leadership Skills: Thomas Barta" (*The Whole Marketer Podcast*, episode 22), accessed 9 December 2020, https://traffic.libsyn.com/ secure/thewholemarketer/Podcast_22_Leadership_2.mp3.

36. Callum Saunders, Head of Planning at Zeal Creative – IPM agency of the year 2019.

37. "Leadership Skills: Thomas Barta" (*The Whole Marketer Podcast*, episode 22), accessed 9 December 2020, https://traffic.libsyn.com/ secure/thewholemarketer/Podcast_22_Leadership_2.mp3.

38. "Commercial: Emma Heal" (*The Whole Marketer Podcast*, episode 3), accessed 9 December 2020, https://traffic.libsyn.com/secure/ thewholemarketer/podcast_3_Commercial.mp3.

39. "Commercial: Emma Heal" (*The Whole Marketer Podcast*, episode 3), accessed 9 December 2020, https://traffic.libsyn.com/secure/ thewholemarketer/podcast_3_Commercial.mp3.

40. "Commercial: Emma Heal" (*The Whole Marketer Podcast*, episode 3), accessed 9 December 2020, https://traffic.libsyn.com/secure/ thewholemarketer/podcast_3_Commercial.mp3.

41. "Insight: Richard Bambrick" (*The Whole Marketer Podcast*, episode 11), accessed 9 December 2020, https://traffic.libsyn.com/secure/ thewholemarketer/podcast_11_Insight__1.mp3.

42. "Insight: Julian Watson" (*The Whole Marketer Podcast*, episode 13), accessed 9 December 2020, https://soundcloud.com/user-587198644/ episode-13-insight-with-guest.

43. See "Strategyzer's Value Proposition Canvas Explained" (Strategyzer), last modified 7 March 2017, https://www.youtube.com/ watch?v=ReM1uqmVfP0.

44. "Insight: Julian Watson" (*The Whole Marketer Podcast*, episode 13), accessed 9 December 2020, https://soundcloud.com/user-587198644/ episode-13-insight-with-guest.

45. Philip Graves, "Everybody Lies: The Importance of Psychological Validity in Consumer Insight," in *Eat Your Greens: Fact-Based Thinking to Improve Your Brand's Health*, ed. Wiemer Snijders (Kibworth Beauchamp: Matador, 2018).

46. Daniel Kahneman, *Thinking, Fast and Slow* (London: Penguin, 2012).

47. Philip Jordanov, "Thinking fast? Slow down." (Neurofied Brain & Behaviour Academy), accessed 24 March 2021, https://neurofied.com/thinking-fast-slow-down/.

48. "Behavioural Science: Kate Socker" (*The Whole Marketer Podcast*, episode 14), accessed 9 December 2020, https://traffic.libsyn.com/secure/thewholemarketer/Podcast_14_Science.mp3.

49. "Behavioural Science: Kate Socker" (*The Whole Marketer Podcast*, episode 14), accessed 9 December 2020, https://traffic.libsyn.com/secure/thewholemarketer/Podcast_14_Science.mp3.

UNIT 2: SOFT SKILLS AND LEADERSHIP SKILLS

1. "Sherilyn Shackell" (*The Whole Marketer Podcast*, episode 21), accessed 9 December 2020, https://traffic.libsyn.com/secure/thewholemarketer/Podcast_21.mp3.

2. "Pete Markey CMO Boots UK" (*The Whole Marketer Podcast*, episode 20), accessed 1 January 2020, https://traffic.libsyn.com/secure/thewholemarketer/Podcast_20_CMO_1.mp3.

3. "Behavioural Science: Kate Socker" (*The Whole Marketer Podcast*, episode 14), accessed 9 December 2020, https://traffic.libsyn.com/secure/thewholemarketer/Podcast_14_Science.mp3

4. "Global Leadership and Innovation: Shweta Harit" (*The Whole Marketer Podcast*, episode 16), accessed 9 December 2020, https://traffic.libsyn.com/secure/thewholemarketer/Podcast_16_Leadership__Innovation_2.mp3.

5. Ken Robinson, *Out of Our Minds: Learning to be Creative* (Hoboken: John Wiley & Sons, 2011).

6. "Consumer Behaviour: Meredith O'Shaughnessy" (*The Whole Marketer Podcast*, episode 2), accessed 9 December 2020, https://traffic.libsyn.com/secure/thewholemarketer/podcast_2_Consumer_Behaviour.mp3.

7. "Storytelling: Anthony 'Tas' Tasgal" (*The Whole Marketer Podcast*, episode 7), accessed 9 December 2020, https://traffic.libsyn.com/secure/thewholemarketer/podcast_7_storytelling.mp3.

8. Edward de Bono, *Six Thinking Hats* (London: Penguin Life, 2016).

9. "Creativity: Shelford Chandler" (*The Whole Marketer Podcast*, episode 19), accessed 9 December 2020, https://traffic.libsyn.com/secure/thewholemarketer/Podcast_19.mp3.

10. Edward de Bono, *Six Thinking Hats* (London: Penguin Life, 2016).

11. "Storytelling: Anthony 'Tas' Tasgal" (*The Whole Marketer Podcast*, episode 7), accessed 9 December 2020, https://traffic.libsyn.com/secure/thewholemarketer/podcast_7_storytelling.mp3.

12. "Leadership Skills: Thomas Barta" (*The Whole Marketer Podcast*, episode 22), accessed 9 December 2020, traffic.libsyn.com/secure/thewholemarketer/Podcast_22_Leadership_2.mp3.

13. "Leadership: Katherine Whitton, CMO Specsavers" (*The Whole Marketer Podcast*, episode 12), https://thewholemarketer.libsyn.com/episode-12-leadership-with-guest-katherine-whitton.

14. "Leadership Skills: Thomas Barta" (*The Whole Marketerr Podcast*, episode 22), accessed 9 December 2020, https://traffic.libsyn.com/secure/thewholemarketer/Podcast_22_Leadership_2.mp3.

15. Simon Sinek, *Leaders Eat Last* (New York: Portfolio, 2014).

16. "Leadership Skills: Thomas Barta" (*The Whole Marketer Podcast*, episode 22), accessed 9 December 2020, https://traffic.libsyn.com/secure/thewholemarketer/Podcast_22_Leadership_2.mp3.

17. "Conviction: Anthony Fletcher CEO Graze.com" (*The Whole Marketer Podcast*, episode 4), accessed 9 December 2020, https://traffic.libsyn.com/secure/thewholemarketer/podcast_4_Conviction.mp3.

18. Anthony Tasgal, *The Storytelling Book* (London: LID Publishing, 2015).

19. "Storytelling: Anthony 'Tas' Tasgal" (*The Whole Marketer Podcast*, episode 7), accessed 9 December 2020, https://traffic.libsyn.com/secure/thewholemarketer/podcast_7_storytelling.mp3.

20. "Storytelling: Anthony 'Tas' Tasgal" (*The Whole Marketer Podcast*, episode 7), accessed 9 December 2020, https://traffic.libsyn.com/secure/thewholemarketer/podcast_7_storytelling.mp3.

21. "Storytelling: Anthony 'Tas' Tasgal" (*The Whole Marketer Podcast*, episode 7), accessed 9 December 2020, https://traffic.libsyn.com/secure/thewholemarketer/podcast_7_storytelling.mp3.

22. "Commitment: Peter Docker" (*The Whole Marketer Podcast*, episode 10), accessed 9 December 2020, https://traffic.libsyn.com/secure/thewholemarketer/Podcast_10_commitment_2.mp3.

23. "Global Leadership and Innovation: Shweta Harit" (*The Whole Marketer Podcast*, episode 16), accessed 9 December 2020, https://traffic.libsyn.com/secure/thewholemarketer/Podcast_16_Leadership__Innovation_2.mp3.

24. "Conviction: Anthony Fletcher CEO Graze.com" (*The Whole Marketer Podcast*, episode 4), accessed 9 December 2020, https://traffic.libsyn.com/secure/thewholemarketer/podcast_4_Conviction.mp3.

25. "Resilience: Alice Ter Haar" (*The Whole Marketer Podcast*, episode 1), accessed 9 December 2020, https://traffic.libsyn.com/secure/thewholemarketer/podcast_1_resiliance.mp3.

26. *Mastering Resilience: Future Focus Toolkit* (Wellbeing Project, 2019), accessed 9 December 2020, https://thewellbeingproject.co.uk/wp-content/uploads/2019/06/Wraw-Future-Focus-Toolkit-Booklet-DIGITAL.pdf.

27. "Competencies: Gemma Butler, Marketing Director CIM" (*The Whole Marketer Podcast*, episode 8), accessed 9 December 2020, https://traffic.libsyn.com/secure/thewholemarketer/Podcast_8_Compentencies_2.mp3.

28. "Leadership: Katherine Whitton, CMO Specsavers" (*The Whole Marketer Podcast*, episode 12), accessed 9 December 2020, https://traffic.libsyn.com/secure/thewholemarketer/Podcast_12_Leadership.mp3.

29. "Situational Leadership" (Center for Leadership Studies), accessed 9 December 2020, https://situational.com/situational-leadership.

30. Thomas Barta and Patrick Barwise, *The 12 Powers of a Marketing Leader: How to Succeed by Building Customer and Company Value* (New York: McGraw-Hill, 2016).

31. More information can be found at www.marketingleader.org. Thomas Barta was a guest on *The Whole Marketer* podcast and kindly provided a worksheet for all listeners, which can be found at

https://labyrinthmarketing.co.uk/wp-content/uploads/2020/11/The-12-powers-of-a-marketing-leader-Ch1.pdf.

32. "Pete Markey CMO Boots UK" (*The Whole Marketer Podcast*, episode 20), accessed 1 January 2020, https://traffic.libsyn.com/secure/thewholemarketer/Podcast_20_CMO_1.mp3.

33. "Professional Marketing Competencies" (The Chartered Institute of Marketing), accessed 9 December 2020, https://www.cim.co.uk/membership/professional-marketing-competencies.

34. "Competencies: Gemma Butler, Marketing Director CIM" (*The Whole Marketer Podcast*, episode 8), accessed 9 December 2020, https://traffic.libsyn.com/secure/thewholemarketer/Podcast_8_Compentencies_2.mp3.

35. See https://thewholemarketer.libsyn.com.

36. "Competencies: Gemma Butler, Marketing Director CIM" (*The Whole Marketer Podcast*, episode 8), accessed 9 December 2020, https://traffic.libsyn.com/secure/thewholemarketer/Podcast_8_Compentencies_2.mp3.

37. "Pete Markey CMO Boots UK" (*The Whole Marketer Podcast*, episode 20), accessed 1 January 2020, https://traffic.libsyn.com/secure/thewholemarketer/Podcast_20_CMO_1.mp3.

38. "Sherilyn Shackell" (*The Whole Marketer Podcast*, episode 21), accessed 9 December 2020, https://traffic.libsyn.com/secure/thewholemarketer/Podcast_21.mp3.

39. "Pete Markey CMO Boots UK" (*The Whole Marketer Podcast*, episode 20), accessed 1 January 2020, https://traffic.libsyn.com/secure/thewholemarketer/Podcast_20_CMO_1.mp3.

UNIT 3: PERSONAL UNDERSTANDING

1. Mary Portas, *Work Like a Woman: A Manifesto for Change* (London: Bantam Press, 2018).

2. "Sherilyn Shackell" (*The Whole Marketer Podcast*, episode 21), accessed 9 December 2020, https://traffic.libsyn.com/secure/thewholemarketer/Podcast_21.mp3.

3. Brené Brown, *Rising Strong* (London: Vermilion, 2015).

4. Quoted in Oprah Winfrey, *The Path Made Clear: Discovering Your Life's Direction and Purpose* (London: Bluebird, 2019).

5. Oprah Winfrey, *The Path Made Clear: Discovering Your Life's Direction and Purpose* (London: Blue Bird, 2019).

6. "The 16 MBTI® Types" (The Myers & Briggs Foundation), accessed 9 December 2020, https://www.myersbriggs.org/my-mbti-personality-type/mbti-basics/the-16-mbti-types.htm.

7. See "Calling All Skeptics: A Look into DiSC® Research" (The Fruitful Toolbox), last modified 6 March 2020, https://thefruitfultoolbox.com/calling-skeptics-look-disc-research.

8. Oprah Winfrey, *The Path Made Clear: Discovering Your Life's Direction and Purpose* (London: Bluebird, 2019).

9. Oprah Winfrey, *The Path Made Clear: Discovering Your Life's Direction and Purpose* (London: Bluebird, 2019).

10. "Commercial: Emma Heal" (*The Whole Marketer Podcast*, episode 3), accessed 9 December 2020, https://traffic.libsyn.com/secure/thewholemarketer/podcast_3_Commercial.mp3.

11. "Flex Appeal," Mother Pukka, accessed 3 February 2021, https://www.motherpukka.co.uk/flex/.

12. Rebecca Gowler, "60% of workers unhappy in their jobs," HR Magazine, accessed 3 February 2021, https://www.hrmagazine.co.uk/article-details/60-of-uk-workers-unhappy-in-their-jobs.

13. "Values in the Workplace: Alex Hirst" (*The Whole Marketer* podcast, Episode 9), accessed 9 December 2020, https://traffic.libsyn.com/secure/thewholemarketer/Podcast_9_Values_in_Workplace_1.mp3.

14. Simon Sinek, David Mead and Peter Docker, *Find Your Why* (London: Portfolio, 2017).

15. Quoted in Viktor E. Frankel, *Man's Search for Meaning* (Boston: Beacon Press, 2014).

16. "Commitment: Peter Docker" (*The Whole Marketer Podcast*, episode 10), accessed 9 December 2020, https://traffic.libsyn.com/secure/thewholemarketer/Podcast_10_commitment_2.mp3.

17. Tony Robbins, "Why We Do What We Do" (TED 2006), accessed 9 December 2020, https://www.ted.com/talks/tony_robbins_why_we_do_what_we_do?language=en.

18. Rhonda Byrne, *The Secret* (London: Simon & Schuster, 2006).

19. Tony Robbins, "Where Focus Goes, Energy Flows" (Tony Robbins), accessed 9 December 2020, https://www.tonyrobbins.com/career-business/where-focus-goes-energy-flows.

20. Eric Berne, *Transactional Analysis in Psychotherapy: A Systematic Individual and Social Psychiatry* (Mansfield Centre, CT: Martino Publishing, 2015).

21. Jo Owen, *The Mindset of Success: From Good Management to Great Leadership* (London: Kogan Page, 2015).

22. Team Tony, "The 2-Millimeter Rule: How Small Changes Can Bring Massive Results" (Tony Robbins), accessed 9 December 2020, https://www.tonyrobbins.com/stories/business-mastery/2-millimeter-rule.

23. Mel Robbins, *The 5 Second Rule: The Surprisingly Simple Way to Live, Love, and Speak with Courage* (Post Hill Press, 2017).

24. A saying common to multiple cultures.

25. Gabrielle Bernstein, *The Universe Has Your Back: How to Feel Safe and Trust Your Life No Matter What* (Carlsbad: Hay House, 2016).

26. Anthony Robbins, *Money – Master the Game: 7 Simple Steps to Financial Freedom* (London: Simon & Schuster, 2014).

27. Jim Rohn, (Business insider n.d.)

28. Jim Rohn, (Business insider n.d.)

ABOUT THE AUTHOR

ABIGAIL DIXON is an award-winning chartered marketer, a fellow of the Chartered Institute of Marketing (CIM), an accredited consultant, a course director and trainer, and an accredited International Coaching Federation coach.

Abigail's mission, purpose and passion are oriented around growing and empowering the people behind brands and businesses. She does this through her unique blend of proven marketing expertise, coaching credentials and passion to empower others to achieve. Her distinctive approach is brought to life as the host of the fortnightly *Whole Marketer* podcast, where she interviews industry and marketing leaders: **www.thewholemarketer.com**

Abigail's unique experience – both first-hand as a client-side marketer and subsequently as a consultant, trainer and coach – means she deeply understands the technical and soft skills required to be a leading marketer in the ever-changing landscape in which marketers now practise. Moreover, she perceives the importance of understanding yourself as a person – what you value, your goals and what is stopping you from achieving them – so you can have a fulfilled life and career.

Known for being honest, authentic and relatable, Abigail speaks openly from the heart about her experiences in daily practice, connecting her professional life with her personal life to inspire listeners to take both individual and collective action to boost their development and growth.

Abigail's marketing calibre is recognized by her peers. She has been an awards judge for multiple industry bodies, namely the CIM, Women in Marketing, the Institute of Promotional Marketing (IPM) and Brand Licensing Europe. She also provides training, consultation and thought leadership for influential marketing bodies, such as the CIM, the IPM and AAR Group, and she consults on the education programme of the IPM. She has trained thousands of marketers over the past decade, both on professional qualifications courses and in-house on a variety of technical skills. The brands and businesses she has worked with in-house include Barclays, Bayer, Beiersdorf, Campari, Coca-Cola, Gilead Sciences, intu, Olympus, Pizza Hut and Xerox.

A trusted coach and voice for empowerment, Abigail has written for a diverse range of media, including the global platform *The Female Lead* and the UK's *Stylist* magazine.

Abigail's over 20 years of marketing experience span multiple sectors and markets, and have included many global household brands, initially on the client side and then in a consultancy capacity. These brands include Bosch, the British Council, Britvic, Burger King, Ferrero, GSK, Pepsi and Premier Foods, to name a few.

Having advised numerous brands and businesses on their long-term strategy, Abigail has proven her ability to turn around brands, delivering sustainable growth with positive return on investment.

In 2015 Abigail founded the award-winning Labyrinth Marketing, a strategic marketing and capability consultancy that helps a variety of brands and businesses across multiple sectors. Having been on the 'other side,' in client-side roles, Abigail wanted to offer consultancy that was markedly different – that understood the genuine needs of marketers, providing a service from marketers for marketers. Labyrinth Marketing not only helps brands and businesses to develop long-term strategies but also provides support to bring these plans to life through training, coaching, mentoring and additional resource.

Highly regarded in the marketing community, Abigail has won various accolades. In recognition of her open approach to mentorship, she was recognized in the Top 50 Kindness Leaders 2020. In 2019, Abigail won Independent Consultant of the Year at the Global Women in Marketing Awards. Labyrinth Marketing won Best Marketing Agency 2018 at the BoC Marketing and PR Brilliance Awards.

For those seeking inspiration and empowerment, Abigail promotes the importance of taking control of your life as a whole, so that all of its aspects are working in harmony and are happening *for* you, not *to* you. She openly and passionately shares her experiences and aims to inspire her audience on how to build a life by design, the benefits of gaining a deeper understanding of who you are and what you need, defining your goals, and addressing the beliefs that you have that are holding you back. She aspires to empower her audience to make this happen.

If you need help owning your marketing role
and career, then please do reach out to Abby at
www.thewholemarketer.com